CONTEMPORARY SCHOOL MATHEMATICS

# Sets and Logic 2

The full scheme comprises:

CONTEMPORARY SCHOOL MATHEMATICS

The St. Dunstan's College Booklets
General Editor: Geoffrey Matthews

# Sets and Logic 2

## C. A. R. BAILEY

EDWARD ARNOLD
London

First published 1964
Reprinted 1965, 1967, 1971

ISBN 0 7131 1295 6

# Contemporary School Mathematics

"Multiply £29 13s. 6½d. by 37."

"Simplify $\dfrac{3x^2+5}{x^2-5x+6} - \dfrac{7x^2+4x+1}{x^2-9x+14}$"

"Prove that the base-angles of an isosceles triangle are equal."

These types of question no longer represent mathematics. In fact, much of the "mathematics" traditionally taught in schools is moribund and due for reform. This does not, however, mean that everything familiar should be scrapped indiscriminately. The C.S.M. booklets point to possible changes in the syllabus, but at the same time show how the existing one can be enlivened with contemporary ideas. They are to supplement rather than replace existing texts, which can still be used with discretion.

Children who "don't like mathematics" can have a change of heart when they see its relevance to the present day. Some time spent on topics such as computers and statistics is therefore not "wasted" even in terms of "O" level passes. Again, the language of sets and the use of matrices help to show mathematics for what it is—a coherent subject with many applications, and *not* a collection of isolated techniques.

The booklets have been written by members of the staff of St. Dunstan's College. The first set has been used with pupils from 11 to 13 and the second with classes up to "O" level standard. They have grown naturally out of class-room experience to the point where a new examination, based on the Outline (inside front cover), seemed desirable. This has been approved by the Oxford and Cambridge Schools Examination Board, and special "O" level papers on this St. Dunstan's syllabus are being set starting in July 1964.

Schools of all types are beginning to experiment in reforming the mathematics syllabus. The C.S.M. booklets are designed to help in this task.

G.M.

# Sets and Logic 2

This sequel to *Sets and Logic 1* extends the applications of Boolean algebra introduced in the earlier volume, and introduces the reader to the concept of a mathematical structure as a set of axioms from which deductions are made by logical argument.

The first two chapters provide an interesting application of such an algebraic structure as a mathematical model for certain aspects of the behaviour of electrical circuits: it is pointed out that such a model is "useful" for as long as it produces results which are valid in the real world. Another such model appears in Chapter III, where an attempt is made to show that a structure based on the language of sets can provide a foundation for the rather hazy idea of probability.

Chapter IV discusses certain important types of relation, and investigates rather informally how these ideas may be used to place the systems of the integers and the rational numbers on an axiomatic footing. Many problems are openly avoided and many others secretly ignored. It is hoped that the thoughtful pupil will spot some of these for himself, and may be led to consult more advanced texts on the subject.

The final chapter discusses some of the basic ideas of logical thought, hitherto largely unconscious. Some emphasis is put on the meaning of the symbols $\Rightarrow$ and $\Leftrightarrow$, but the formal and manipulative aspects of the topic are not carried too far. A re-reading of Chapter IV in the light of Chapter V is a valuable exercise.

# CONTENTS

7

## ACKNOWLEDGEMENTS

I am greatly indebted to Dr. J. V. Armitage and Dr. J. Shoesmith of the University of Durham for their penetrating and valuable criticisms of the manuscript. Any illogicalities that remain have not been overlooked by them, but are rather left because their discussion requires a sophistication perhaps inappropriate to the maturity of the prospective reader.

## CHAPTER I

# Switching Algebra

When buying replacements for household electrical equipment, we have to make certain numerical specifications: we may require a 240-volt, 150-watt lamp, or a 15-amp three-pin plug. If we get these quantities wrong, the equipment will work inefficiently or not at all. These matters are important, but even when we have attended to them, we still have to switch on the light. Even this may not be enough if we have forgotten to switch on at the mains. This chapter will be concerned only with the results of inserting switches into a circuit, and the converse problem of what switches are required to achieve a desired result. We shall assume that all questions of power, voltage, etc., have already been satisfactorily settled, and concentrate entirely on the switches.

This enormous simplification of the problem is typical of any practical application of mathematics: when calculating the sizes of the pieces of metal needed to make a shed, we ignore the fact that metal expands with heat. This is a perfectly sound simplification, provided that we remember that it *is* a simplification, and that we must allow for the expansion of metal when we build a large bridge. A *mathematical model* of a real situation must be as simple as possible provided it is going to give answers correct enough for the purpose in hand. The construction of sound mathematical models is the chief business of the applied mathematician.

To construct our model we shall denote sections of a circuit which are controlled by a switch or system of switches by letters such as $x$, $y$, $z$, etc. As far as we are concerned, either the section $x$ has a current passing through, in which case we write

$$x = 1,$$

or there is no current passing through, in which case we write

$$x = 0.$$

We can show these two situations diagrammatically as follows:

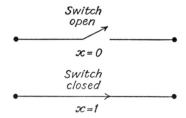

Notice that the diagrams show no battery or return wire: these are not relevant to our discussion, and so we show only the parts of the circuit containing the switches.

Remember that the symbols 0 and 1 are not numbers: the statements $x = 3$ or $x = \frac{1}{2}$ have no meaning in this context. A switch is a two-state device: it is either open or closed, and so only two symbols are needed to describe it.

Now look at this diagram:

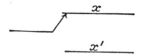

If the switch is in the upper position, as shown, the wire $x$ will pass the current, that is

$$x = 1,$$

and the wire marked $x'$ will be dead, that is

$$x' = 0.$$

If, however, the switch is in the lower position, we have the reverse situation,

$$x = 0$$
$$\text{and } x' = 1.$$

If we allow no intermediate position of the switch, then the state of the wire $x'$ is always opposite to the state of the wire $x$. This symbolism is one we shall always use to denote two wires whose states are always opposite to each other.

Another way of achieving the same result is by means of an electro-magnet, as shown in this diagram:

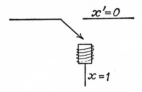

The magnet is controlled by the wire $x$. When $x = 0$ the magnet is off, and a spring keeps the switch closed, so that current can pass through the wire $x'$, that is $x' = 1$ when $x = 0$. On the other hand, when $x = 1$ the magnet pulls the switch open, thus breaking the circuit in the wire $x'$, so that $x' = 0$. Thus $x$ and $x'$ are always in opposite states. The switch here is called a *break-contact*. The next diagram illustrates a *make-contact*:

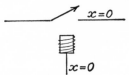

You will see that in this circuit the spring normally keeps the switch open, and the effect of the magnet is to close it. This means that either both wires are carrying current or they are both dead, that is, they are always in the *same* state. When this happens, we denote *both* wires by the same symbol $x$, since the statements $x = 0$ or $x = 1$ will describe the state of both wires simultaneously: if we particularly wish to distinguish between the two, we may call one wire $x$ and the other $y$, and then we would write

$$x = y.$$

The familiar sign of equality must here be taken to mean either that $x = 1$ and $y = 1$ or that $x = 0$ and $y = 0$.

The next diagram shows *two* switches *in series*:

Clearly current will only flow through this circuit if *both* switches are closed. This situation is denoted by the symbol

$$xy.$$

Those of you who have studied Volume 1 will recognise this symbol, when applied to two *sets* x and y, as representing the intersection of the two sets. In that case, an element is a member of the set xy if and only if it is a member of *both x and y*. There is a close analogy between this interpretation and the one we are discussing here, where the circuit xy is carrying current if and only if *both x and y* are carrying current.

The resemblance to the ordinary algebraic multiplication symbol is a fruitful one. Remember that the circuit is only carrying current if both x and y are carrying current: that is, $xy = 1$ only when $x = 1$ and $y = 1$. There are three other cases to consider: either x or y may be dead, or they may both be dead. In all these three cases, $xy = 0$. We can set out these facts in a table:

| x | y | xy |
|---|---|----|
| 0 | 0 | 0 |
| 0 | 1 | 0 |
| 1 | 0 | 0 |
| 1 | 1 | 1 |

At first glance this looks like a simple multiplication table: in fact, it *is* a simple multiplication table, if the symbols stand for numbers. The same table can show either facts about numbers or facts about switches, depending on the interpretation.

EXERCISE 1

1. The following diagram illustrates two switches *in parallel*:

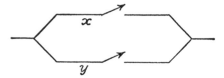

This situation is denoted by the symbol

$$x + y.$$

Complete the following table:

| x | y | x + y |
|---|---|-------|
| 0 | 0 | |
| 0 | 1 | |
| 1 | 0 | |
| 1 | 1 | |

Does this table differ in any way from an ordinary addition table?

2.

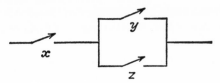

The diagram shows a circuit containing two switches in parallel (and so symbolised by $y + z$) connected in series to another switch in a wire $x$. The complete circuit is therefore symbolised as

$$x(y + z).$$

All three switches are shown open: if various combinations of switches are closed, the complete circuit will pass current in some cases but not in others. Show the various possibilities by completing the following table:

| $x$ | $y$ | $z$ | $x(y + z)$ |
|---|---|---|---|
| 0 | 0 | 0 | 0 |
| 0 | 0 | 1 | 0 |
| 0 | 1 | 0 | |
| 0 | 1 | 1 | |
| 1 | 0 | 0 | |
| 1 | 0 | 1 | |
| 1 | 1 | 0 | |
| 1 | 1 | 1 | |

3.

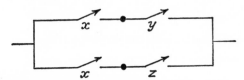

The diagram shows a circuit consisting of $x$ and $y$ in series, and another circuit consisting of $x$ and $z$ in series. These two circuits are connected in parallel. The symbol for the whole circuit will therefore be

$$xy + xz.$$

Using the eight possible combinations of $x$, $y$ and $z$ listed in Q.2, complete a table for

| $x$ | $y$ | $z$ | $xy + xz$ |
|---|---|---|---|
| 0 | 0 | 0 | 0 |

etc.

(Remember that because the same symbol $x$ is used for two different switches, these two switches must be open or closed together.) Compare your table with that in Q.2. What formula can you deduce from these two tables?

4. Draw a diagram of a circuit represented by

$$x + x'.$$

(The $+$ symbol means two switches in parallel.)

Complete the following table:

| $x$ | $x'$ | $x + x'$ |
|-----|------|----------|
| 0   | 1    |          |
| 1   | 0    |          |

(There are no other possibilities, because $x$ and $x'$ must always be in opposite states, by definition.)

5. What is the symbolic statement describing the following circuit?

Complete a table of possibilities similar to that in Q.4.

6. What formula describes the following circuit?

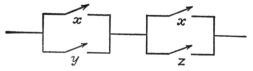

Complete an eight-row table for the circuit similar to those in Qs. 2 and 3.

7. Draw a diagram of the circuit whose formula is

$$x + yz$$

and complete the corresponding table. Compare with the table in Q.6 and deduce a formula.

### Circuit Algebra

You will probably have realised by now that the switching algebra we have been investigating corresponds very closely to the algebra of sets discussed in Volume 1. If you turn to the laws of Boolean algebra listed in the appendix you will see that the work of the last exercise has verified laws 3 and 5, and you should be able to show quite easily that laws 1, 2, 4 and 10 are true by considering the definitions of the various symbols. Law 6 is also a matter of definition. To check the remaining three laws we return to the "addition" and "multiplication" tables we have already met, together with the meaning of the symbol $x'$.

We have seen that the *switching* "multiplication" table exactly resembles the multiplication table for the *numbers* 0 and 1, and that the *switching* "addition" table differs from the addition table of the *numbers* 0 and 1 only in the fact that

$$1 + 1 = 1.$$

Since switching algebra is two-valued, any formula we wish to check requires only that we replace the letters by the symbols 0 and 1 in turn, making sure that we cover all possible combinations. If there are 2 letters, there will be $2 \times 2 = 4$ possibilities, if there are 3 letters, there will be $2^3 = 8$ possibilities (see Exercise 1), and in general, if there are $n$ letters, there will be $2^n$ possibilities.

To check the formula

$$1 + x = 1$$

we construct a simple table:

| $x$ | $1 + x$ |
|-----|---------|
| 0   | 1       |
| 1   | 1       |

using the switching "addition" table, and we find that $1 + x = 1$ in both cases. You should check the rest of laws 7 and 8 in the same way.

To check a formula such as De Morgan's Law

$$(x + y)' = x'y'$$

we need to construct *two* tables, one for the left-hand side and another for the right-hand side, and then we must check that the final columns are identical.

Here is the table for $(x + y)'$

| $x$ | $y$ | $x + y$ | $(x + y)'$ |
|-----|-----|---------|------------|
| 0   | 0   | 0       | 1          |
| 0   | 1   | 1       | 0          |
| 1   | 0   | 1       | 0          |
| 1   | 1   | 1       | 0          |

The first two columns simply list the various possibilities, and the third column is formed by the addition of the first two: the final column lists the complements of the third column. Now we do the same for the formula $x'y'$:

*Sets and Logic 2*

| x | y | x′ | y′ | x′y′ |
|---|---|----|----|------|
| 0 | 0 | 1 | 1 | 1 |
| 0 | 1 | 1 | 0 | 0 |
| 1 | 0 | 0 | 1 | 0 |
| 1 | 1 | 0 | 0 | 0 |

Again the first two columns list the possibilities: the third and fourth columns show the complements of the first two, and the last column is formed from the previous two by multiplication. Since the final columns of the two tables are identical, we have shown that $(x + y)' = x'y'$ for *all* possible combinations of values of $x$ and $y$.

Exercise 2

Verify the following formulae by constructing tables:

(1) $(xy)' = x' + y'$  (2) $x + xy = x$
(3) $x(x + y) = x$  (4) $(xy + x'y')' = xy' + x'y$

### Simplification of Circuits

Now that we have shown that switching algebra is a Boolean algebra we can, of course, apply whatever skill we have acquired in the routine manipulation of a Boolean algebra to simplifying circuits: there is no new technique to learn. The only difference is that when we arrive at a solution in symbols, we interpret it as a circuit instead of as a set. Any mathematical structure such as this which can be interpreted in more than one way is called *polyvalent*. Such a structure is clearly of great importance: the pure mathematician studies the structure for its own sake, but his results can then be taken by the scientist or engineer and applied each to his own field of investigation.

Boolean algebra can be used by the electronic engineer both to design circuits to achieve certain results, and to simplify circuits which are known to achieve certain results. As an example, study the following circuit:

(For simplicity, the switches themselves are not shown.)

This circuit might be used to control the door to a dangerous piece of research equipment. The safety lock on the door cannot be released unless two switches are thrown, one at least of which must be $a$ or $b$. You will see that the circuit cannot close unless two switches are thrown, and even then the combination of $c$ and $d$ will not achieve this.

The whole circuit consists of five smaller circuits in parallel, each smaller circuit containing two switches in series: we can represent the whole circuit by the *Boolean function*

$$ab + ac + ad + bc + bd.$$

This function could be factorised as

$$a(b + c + d) + b(c + d)$$

which represents two circuits in parallel: the first, $a(b + c + d)$, consists of three switches $b$, $c$ and $d$ in parallel, connected to switch $a$ in series, and the second is similar. We can show this new version of the function diagrammatically as follows:

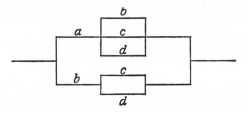

If you study this circuit you will see that it has the same effect as the previous one: it requires the closure of two different switches other than $c$ and $d$ to close the circuit. This circuit, however, contains only seven switches (or make-contacts), whereas the earlier one required ten.

Another way of treating the same function algebraically is to write

$$ab + ac + ad + bc + bd = ab + (a + b)(c + d)$$

(verify this), and the right-hand side of this formula can be translated into a circuit like this:

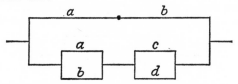

Check for yourself that once again this circuit has the same properties as the original one, but contains only six contacts.

We treated the original Boolean function algebraically in two different ways, each giving us a new circuit with the same properties as the original one: the last proved to be most economical in terms of contacts. This could not have been foreseen when we started: there is no routine process which will inevitably lead to the simplest circuit. This is a matter of trial and ingenuity, and in any case the number of contacts is not the only measure of economy: hence there is not generally one "best" solution to a simplification problem such as this.

EXERCISE 3

(The first four questions are to give practice in the techniques of Boolean algebra, for those who need such practice.)

1. (Based chiefly on the laws 3(i), 4(ii) and 5(ii): see Appendix.) Expand the following and simplify where possible:

    (a) $x(x + y)$    (b) $x(x' + y')$    (c) $xy(x' + y')$    (d) $xy'(x + y)$
    (e) $xy(xy + x'z)$    (f) $(x + y')(x' + y)$    (g) $(xy' + yz)(xz' + y'z')$.

2. (Based chiefly on the laws 3(i) and 5(i).) Factorise and simplify the following: use the fact that $1 + x = 1$ where applicable.

    (a) $xy + xz$    (b) $x' + x'y$    (c) $xy'z + xyz$    (d) $xy' + xy'z'$
    (e) $xy + yz + yz'$.

3. (Based chiefly on the law 3(ii).) Factorise the following:

    (a) $x + yz$    (b) $xy + z$    (c) $x + abc$    (d) $xy' + x'y$    (e) $x + x'y$
    (f) $xy + x'y'$.

4. (Based chiefly on law 9.) Find the complements of the following:

    (a) $(x' + y)$    (b) $xy'$    (c) $xy'z$    (d) $x + yz'$    (e) $(x + y)(x + z')$.

5. Interpret the following circuit in symbols: simplify the results by Boolean algebra and draw the new equivalent circuit:

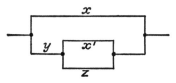

(Notice that the switch $z$ turns out to be unnecessary.)

6. Interpret the following circuit in symbols:

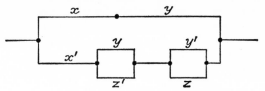

7. Complete the following table for the circuit $y(x + z) + x'y'z'$

| x | y | z | x' | y' | z' | x + z | y(x + z) | x'y'z' | y(x + z) +x'y'z' |
|---|---|---|----|----|----|-------|----------|--------|------------------|
| 0 | 0 | 0 | 1 | 1 | 1 | 0 | 0 | 1 | 1 |
| 0 | 0 | 1 | 1 | 1 | 0 | 1 | 0 | 0 | 0 |
| 0 | 1 | 0 | 1 | 0 | 1 | 0 | 0 | 0 | |
| 0 | 1 | 1 | 1 | 0 | 0 | 1 | | | |
| 1 | 0 | 0 | | | | | | | |
| 1 | 0 | 1 | | | | | | | |
| 1 | 1 | 0 | | | | | | | |
| 1 | 1 | 1 | | | | | | | |

8. Make a table for your symbolic interpretation of the circuit in Q.6 similar to the table in Q.7. Verify that the two circuits are equivalent. Also show their equivalence by using Boolean algebra.

9. Draw the circuit given in Q.7. Draw also the circuit $(y + x'z')$ $(x + z + y')$. Verify by algebra that the two circuits are equivalent.

10. Interpret the following circuit in symbols, simplify the result and draw the simplified circuit:

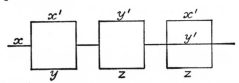

## CHAPTER II

# Designing Circuits

In the last chapter we saw how it was possible to represent a series-parallel circuit as a Boolean function, and, conversely, how to interpret a Boolean function as a series-parallel circuit. (We may use the word "function" here because once we have assigned particular values, 0 or 1, to each letter in the expression, then the expression itself can take only one possible value. This use of the word is an extension of the definition given in *Sets and Logic 1*, Chapter V.) Take as an example the function which we will represent by the letter $f$, and which is defined by the formula

$$f = (x + y)(x' + y').$$

If we assign various values to $x$ and to $y$, we can calculate the corresponding (unique) values of $f$, as in the following table:

| $x$ $y$ | $x'$ $y'$ | $x + y$ | $x' + y'$ | $f$ |
|---|---|---|---|---|
| 0  0 | 1  1 | 0 | 1 | 0 |
| 0  1 | 1  0 | 1 | 1 | 1 |
| 1  0 | 0  1 | 1 | 1 | 1 |
| 1  0 | 0  0 | 1 | 0 | 0 |

The circuit can be drawn diagrammatically like this:

or, more realistically, as in the next diagram, which shows a battery, a light to represent the function (the light will be on when the function has the value 1), and the state of the switches when $x = 0$ and $y = 1$:

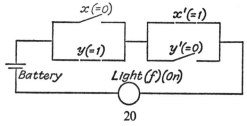

20

We can use Boolean algebra to get an alternative version of the same function:

$$f = (x + y)(x' + y')$$
$$= xx' + xy' + yx' + yy'$$
$$= xy' + yx'$$

Examine this formula for $f$ carefully: it tells us that $f = 1$ in two different cases,

EITHER $x = 1$ and $y = 0$ (so that $y' = 1$)
OR $x = 0$ and $y = 1$.

If we return to the table on the previous page, we see that this is indeed the case: $f = 1$ in the second and third rows of the table only, where $x$ and $y$ have the values just mentioned. This means that, if we had not known the formula for $f$, we could have deduced it provided that we were given that $f = 1$ in the second and third rows of the table only, thus:

| $x$ | $y$ | $f$ |
|-----|-----|-----|
| 0 | 0 | 0 |
| 0 | 1 | 1 |
| 1 | 0 | 1 |
| 1 | 1 | 0 |

We would argue as follows:

$f = 1$ either when $x = 0$ and $y = 1$, that is when $x'y = 1$, or when $x = 1$ and $y = 0$, that is when $xy' = 1$, so $f = x'y + xy'$,

as we have already seen. We could then use Boolean algebra if we wished to transform this formula to the one representing the circuit we have already drawn.

Under what circumstances would we want to design this circuit? One simple application is the light which many houses have in the hall, controlled by two switches, one by the front door ($x$) and the other by the kitchen or sitting-room ($y$). Suppose everyone is out, and that both switches and the light are off, that is, $x = y = f = 0$, as in the top row of the above table. The housewife comes home from shopping on a winter afternoon, switches on at the door ($x = 1$) and the light goes on ($f = 1$). We are now in the third row of the table. She goes into the kitchen, turning the switch ON there, and the light goes OFF (now $x = 1$, $y = 1$ and $f = 0$, as in the last row of the table). When her husband comes in, he switches OFF at the front door, and the light goes ON. This is represented by the second row of the table and completes the possibilities. So we can use the circuit discussed to control this hall light, either in the form already drawn on p. 20 or in the form

$$f = xy' + x'y$$

which can be drawn as under:

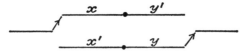

Switches which act as indicated in this diagram are called *transfer* switches.

EXERCISE 1

1. It is required to construct a function $f$ which has the values indicated by the following table:

| $x$ | $y$ | $f$ |
|---|---|---|
| 0 | 0 | 0 |
| 0 | 1 | 1 |
| 1 | 0 | 1 |
| 1 | 1 | 1 |

From the second row of the table, one term of the function is $x'y$. There will be three terms altogether. Write down the complete formula for $f$, and use Boolean algebra to show that this can be simplified to $f = x + y$.

2. A function is designated by the following table:

| $x$ | $y$ | $z$ | $f$ |
|---|---|---|---|
| 0 | 0 | 0 | 0 |
| 0 | 0 | 1 | 1 |
| 0 | 1 | 0 | 0 |
| 0 | 1 | 1 | 0 |
| 1 | 0 | 0 | 0 |
| 1 | 0 | 1 | 0 |
| 1 | 1 | 0 | 1 |
| 1 | 1 | 1 | 1 |

Write down a formula for $f$. Simplify this expression by factorising two of the terms and using the fact that

$$z + z' = 1.$$

Draw the resulting circuit.

3. Construct a table similar to that in Q.2 for a light controlled by three switches, such that the light will be on if and only if an odd number of switches are on. Write down the Boolean function for the circuit, simplify it if possible, and draw your circuit.

4. Design as simple a circuit as possible for a light which will go on only when at least two out of three controlling switches are on.

5. A safety device on a machine is controlled by four switches, *a*, *b*, *c* and *d*. Each switch is thrown when the corresponding part of the machine fails. The device turns the machine off altogether when *a* is thrown or when any two of the others are thrown. Design the necessary circuit.

### Gates

In many practical circuits the switches are controlled, not by hand, but by electromagnetic relays or other more sophisticated devices. One such simple device was shown on p. 11. The purpose of this particular device was, roughly speaking, to produce $x'$ from $x$. We reproduce the diagram here.

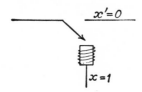

The wire marked $x'$ has its own source of current, and will carry a signal (that is $x' = 1$) so long as the wire $x$ is dead and the magnet is inactive, leaving the switch closed. The wire $x$ is called the input of this device, and the wire $x'$ is called the output. Any device that has this effect, that is, that the output is opposite to the input, is called an *inverter*.*
The exact method of operation of the device is usually unimportant in the design of the circuit, and so it is represented by a symbol as follows:

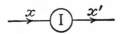

An arrow has to be drawn to distinguish between the input and the output.

* Other terms are also used.

In exactly the same way, a device can be made with two inputs, $x$ and $y$, such that there will only be an output signal if *both x and y* carry a signal. Such a device is called an *and-gate*, and naturally the output is denoted by $xy$, since it will correspond to the type of series circuit we have been discussing. We shall represent an and-gate by the following symbol:

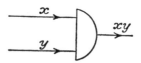

There is only one other device of this type which we shall discuss here, and that is the *or-gate*. You will have guessed that this device also has two inputs $x$ and $y$, and that the output carries a signal if either *x or y* (or both) carries a signal, so that the output can be symbolised by $x + y$. We shall use the following symbol for an or-gate:

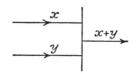

### EXERCISE 2

Show how an and-gate and an or-gate can be constructed by using electromagnetic relays, as in the inverter.

### Circuits using gates

The circuit discussed on p. 21 to control a hall light from two switches can be very simply constructed using transfer switches, as in the diagram on p. 22. Purely as an illustration, we now see how to construct it with the aid of gates. The corresponding function is

$$f = xy' + x'y.$$

This function contains two complements (dashes), for which we shall require two inverters: two products, requiring two and-gates; and one sum, requiring an or-gate. The circuit can be drawn as in the diagram below:

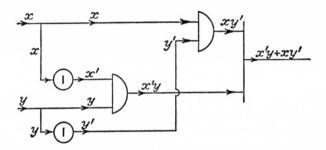

Notice how we can incorporate both $x$ and $x'$, say, in the same circuit by running an extra lead from $x$ through an inverter. This simple device can of course be used to produce, not just the complement of $x$ or of $y$, but the complement of, say, $xy' + x'y$ itself, by running a lead from the right-hand end of the above circuit through an inverter, as indicated below:

$$f = x'y + xy'$$

$$f' = (x'y + xy')'$$

Using De Morgan's laws (see Appendix), we have

$$
\begin{aligned}
f' &= (xy' + x'y)' \\
&= (xy')'(x'y)' \\
&= (x' + y)(x + y') \\
&= x'x + x'y' + xy + yy' \\
&= xy + x'y'
\end{aligned}
$$

In this way, if a particular circuit contains both the expressions

$$xy' + x'y$$
$$\text{and } xy + x'y'$$

we can, having constructed a circuit for the first expression, obtain the second simply by leading the first through an inverter, instead of starting again from scratch.

1. Work again through Exercise 1, Q.3, and show that the Boolean function for a circuit controlling a light from three switches, such that the light is on if and only if an odd number of switches are on, is

$$f = z(xy + x'y') + z'(xy' + x'y).$$

Since this circuit contains a part represented by $xy' + x'y$ which we have already drawn on p. 25, and also a part represented by $xy + x'y'$, which we have seen is simply the complement of $xy' + x'y$, draw the circuit on p. 25 again and extend it to solve the three-switch problem.

2. Using the fact that $ab' + a'b = (a + b)(a' + b')$ and also the law $(a' + b') = (ab)'$, show how the function

$$f = ab' + a'b$$

can be realised as a circuit containing only four gates instead of the five shown on p. 25.

3. Show that the function describing a circuit to control a light such that the light is on if and only if exactly two of the switches $a$, $b$ and $c$ are on can be written as

$$f = abc' + c(ab' + a'b).$$

Constructing the part of the circuit $ab' + a'b$ as in Q.2, draw the complete circuit.

## Computer Circuits

So far we have been using the *symbols* 1 and 0 to indicate whether a particular wire is carrying current or not. Of course, it is equally simple to reverse the interpretation and to represent the *number* 1 by a wire carrying current and the *number* 0 by a wire which is not carrying current. But since these are the only possible states of a wire, it appears that we may only represent the numbers 0 and 1 in this way. To make this system useful, we must find a method of representing larger numbers using only the symbols 0 and 1. The method used is called the *binary system*.

We can illustrate this system by taking the four aces from a pack of cards, and laying them face down in a row, thus:

This will represent the number 0, which we can write symbolically as

0000.

We then work according to the following rules:

(a) To put another 1 into the system we turn over the right-hand card.

(b) Whenever a card is turned from face-*up* to face-*down*, the next card on the *left* is also turned.

At the moment our cards represent 0. To represent 1, we must put another 1 into the system, for which we use rule (a), giving us

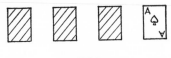

or 0001.

To represent 2, we must put another 1 in, so by rule (a) we turn over the right-hand card. Since this card will be turning from face-up to face-down, we must apply rule (b) and turn the next card also, giving us

or 0010.

To represent 3, we turn the right-hand card again, giving (in symbols)

0011.

To represent 4, we turn the right-hand card yet again, and since rule (b) applies, the next card is also turned: rule (b) applies yet again, so we turn the next one also, finally getting

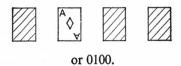

or 0100.

Another turn gives us 0101, representing 5, and so on. So far we have shown the following:

| | |
|---|---|
| 0 | 0000 |
| 1 | 0001 |
| 2 | 0010 |
| 3 | 0011 |
| 4 | 0100 |
| 5 | 0101 |

### EXERCISE 4

1. Continue this table as far as possible. What is the greatest number we can represent by four cards or digits 0 and 1?

2. What is the greatest number we could represent if we only used two digits? Or if we only used three digits? What do you think would be the greatest number we could represent if we used five digits?

3. Represent the following numbers in the binary* system:

(a) 17       (b) 24       (c) 36.

4. What ordinary numbers do these binary numbers represent?

(a) 1010      (b) 11001      (c) 10110.

Now we shall see how to design a logical circuit to perform the simplest operation of all in arithmetic—the addition of two numbers, each of which may be either 0 or 1. We shall symbolise these numbers by the letters $x$ and $y$, and the four possibilities, together with the required results, are shown in the following table:

| $x$ | $y$ | total |
|---|---|---|
| 0 | 0 | 0 |
| 0 | 1 | 1 |
| 1 | 0 | 1 |
| 1 | 1 | 10 |

We see at once that our circuit must have two outputs, since the last row of the table requires two digits to represent the total: we shall call these outputs the sum digit and the carry digit (which will be zero except in the last row) and refer to them by the letters $s$ and $c$ respectively. We can now rewrite the table as follows:

* For a fuller discussion on binary numbers see Lovis, *Computers 1*.

| x | y | c | s |
|---|---|---|---|
| 0 | 0 | 0 | 0 |
| 0 | 1 | 0 | 1 |
| 1 | 0 | 0 | 1 |
| 1 | 1 | 1 | 0 |

Using the methods discussed earlier in this chapter, we can write

$$c = xy$$
$$s = x'y + xy'$$

The carry digit $c$ can be realised by the use of an and-gate, and the sum digit $s$ has already appeared on p. 25, where the diagram shows five gates in use. However, $s$ can be simplified by the use of Boolean algebra, as follows:

$$s = x'y + xy'$$
$$= (x + y)(x' + y')$$
$$= (x + y)(xy)'$$

and this version requires only four gates: furthermore, in the course of realising this formula for $s$, we shall have the function $xy$ as part of the circuit, which will also supply the carry digit $c$. The final circuit can be drawn thus:

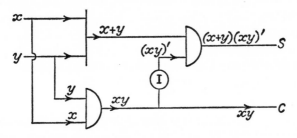

EXERCISE 5

1. When adding two numbers together, each step after the first may require the addition of *three* digits, since there may be a digit carried from the previous column of addition. Thus a circuit to add two numbers should in general have three inputs, one for each digit in the current column and one for the digit carried from the previous column. Such a device is known as a *full adder*, as opposed to the circuit just discussed in the text, which is known as a *half adder*. If we represent these inputs

by the letters $x$, $y$ and $a$, we have the following table showing the required outputs:

| $x$ | $y$ | $a$ | total |
|-----|-----|-----|-------|
| 0 | 0 | 0 | 0 |
| 0 | 0 | 1 | 1 |
| 0 | 1 | 0 | 1 |
| 0 | 1 | 1 | 10 |
| 1 | 0 | 0 | 1 |
| 1 | 0 | 1 | 10 |
| 1 | 1 | 0 | 10 |
| 1 | 1 | 1 | 11 |

It is clear that a carry digit is only required in the fourth, sixth, seventh and eighth rows, and we can represent this by the Boolean function

$$c = x'ya + xy'a + xya' + xya$$
$$= a(x'y + xy') + xy(a + a')$$
$$= a(x'y + xy') + xy \text{ (since } a + a' = 1).$$

If we introduce the symbol $h$ to represent the function $x'y + xy'$, this can be written

$$c = ah + xy.$$

Show in the same way that the sum digit $s$ can be written as

$$s = a'h + ah'.$$

Notice that $h$ is in fact the sum digit of the half-adder circuit discussed in the text, and that the function $s$ above is again the sum digit of the half adder, this time with inputs $a$ and $h$. Using these facts, draw the circuit for the full adder using nine gates.

2. At any stage of a subtraction, we are subtracting a digit $y$ from a digit $x$, possibly having "borrowed one" to enable us to complete the previous stage. We represent this borrowed digit by $a$. The result of the subtraction is a digit $p$ written down, and possibly a digit $q$ has to be borrowed from the next column. The necessary circuit will thus have three inputs and two outputs. The first few lines of the table are given:

| x | y | a | p | q |
|---|---|---|---|---|
| 0 | 0 | 0 | 0 | 0 |
| 0 | 0 | 1 | 1 | 1 |
| 0 | 1 | 0 | 1 | 1 |
| 0 | 1 | 1 | 0 | 1 |

Complete the table, and design as simple a circuit as you can to realise the functions $p$ and $q$. Some of the techniques already used in the half adder and full adder will again be applicable here.

## CHAPTER III

# Sample Spaces and Probability*

In the card game of Bridge, the Aces, Kings, Queens, Jacks and tens are known as honour cards or honours. Let us assume that we have extracted the spade suit from a pack and have laid the thirteen cards of this suit face down on a table. Next we turn over one of the cards: either it is an honour ($h$), or it is not an honour ($n$). This set of two possibilities

$$\{h, n\}$$

is called a *sample space* for the *experiment* of drawing a card from our spade suit. Each of the elements $h$ and $n$ is called a *sample point*.

There are three things to note about this sample space:

(a) it covers all possibilities; every experiment must produce $\{h\}$ or $\{n\}$

(b) the possibilities are mutually exclusive; it is not possible to find a card which is both $\{h\}$ and $\{n\}$

(c) intuitively, we feel that the two events are not equally probable, since there are fewer honours than non-honours.

The last remark (c) shows that the elements of a sample space need not have equal probabilities. The first two properties, (a) and (b) are essential. We might have classified the cards according to whether they carried an odd or an even number of pips, and written down the set of possibilities

$$\{odd, even\}$$

but this does *not* constitute a sample space, since the King, Queen and Jack are not covered in this classification. If we try to cover this difficulty by adopting the classification

$$\{odd, even, honour\}$$

---

* This chapter begins the task of putting the idea of probability on a sound logical footing. For a less formal discussion of the topic see Sherlock, *Introduction to Probability and Statistics*.

this is still *not* a sample space, since the ten of spades is both even and an honour, breaking the condition mentioned in (b) above. If we use the phrase "Court card", to denote a Jack, Queen or King, then the set

$$\{odd, even, Court\ card\}$$

*is* a sample space.

Since the experiment we are discussing consists of drawing one card, a more useful sample space might be the set of sample points

$$S = \{A, 2, 3, 4, 5, 6, 7, 8, 9, 10, J, Q, K\}$$

This set has 13 members. We describe this fact by writing

$$n(S) = 13$$

Other sets we have mentioned are

$$H = \{10, J, Q, K, A\}$$
$$N = \{2, 3, 4, 5, 6, 7, 8, 9\}$$
$$O = \{A, 3, 5, 7, 9\}$$
$$E = \{2, 4, 6, 8, 10\}$$
$$C = \{J, Q, K\}$$

and we have
$$n(H) = 5$$
$$n(N) = 8, \text{ and so on.}$$

Notice that each of these sets has the property that every one of its members is also a member of the sample space $S$ above. This means that they are all *subsets* of $S$, and we write

$$H \subset S$$
$$C \subset S, \text{ and so on.}$$

Any subset of a sample space is called an *event*. Thus an event is an aggregate of sample points. In this example, $S$ represents all the possible cards available for the experiment, and if we draw the 10, then the event $H$ has occurred (and indeed, the event E has occurred also). An event which contains only one sample point, such as the event {10}, is called a *simple* event. Any event with more than one member can be described as the *union* of several simple events: thus the event $C$ above is the union of the three events {J}, {Q} and {K}, and we write

$$C = \{J\} \cup \{Q\} \cup \{K\}$$

The union of two events in general is the event containing all the sample points occurring in either set. Thus

$$N \cup O = \{2, 3, 4, 5, 6, 7, 8, 9, A\}$$

and contains only 9 members, although $n(N) = 8$ and $n(O) = 5$. This is because there are 4 sample points common to both sets. The set formed from these four sample points is called the *intersection* of $N$ and $O$, and we write

$$N \cap O = \{3, 5, 7, 9\}$$

From this discussion we see that

$$n(N \cup O) = n(N) + n(O) - n(N \cap O)$$

and this can be seen to apply to any two sets $A$ and $B$. The number of elements in the union of two sets is the sum of the numbers of elements in each, less the number of elements in their intersection.

It may happen that two sets have no elements in common, such as the sets $E$ and $C$ above. In that case we say that the set $E \cap C$ is *empty*, and we write

$$E \cap C = \varnothing$$

The symbol $\varnothing$ is called the *empty set*. Two sets whose intersection is the empty set are said to be disjoint, and then we have, for two *disjoint* sets $A$ and $B$,

$$n(A \cup B) = n(A) + n(B)$$

### Exercise 1

All the symbols used in this exercise have already been defined in the text.

1. Is $E$ a subset of $N$?
2. Is it true that $C \subset H$?
3. List the sets $E \cup H$ and $E \cap H$: what are $n(E)$, $n(H)$, $n(E \cap H)$, $n(E \cup H)$?
4. Is it true that $(N \cap O) \subset S$? Is it true that $(H \cup E) \subset S$? Is it true that $(H \cap E) \subset S$? Is it true that $(H \cup N) \subset S$? Is it true that $(H \cap N) \subset S$?

### Probability

A *probability* is a number $p$ assigned to an event, such that

$$0 \leqslant p \leqslant 1$$

A *probability model* is a sample space such that
　　(i) each sample point is assigned a probability.
　　(ii) the sum of the probabilities of all the sample points is 1.
　　(iii) the probability of $\varnothing$ is 0.

We define the probability of any other event as the sum of the probabilities of the simple events of which it is the union.

If we return to our sample space $S$, consisting of the spade suit of a pack of cards, we may feel that it is equally likely that any one of the thirteen cards be chosen, and that we must accordingly assign to each element the same probability. This means that each simple event, such as $\{2\}$ or $\{J\}$, must be assigned the probability $\frac{1}{13}$. An event such as $H$, which is the union of five simple events, will then have the probability $\frac{5}{13}$. The event $H \cup E$ is the union of simple events whose number is given by

$$n(H \cup E) = n(H) + n(E) - n(H \cap E)$$
$$= 5 + 5 - 1$$
$$= 9$$

So the probability of drawing an honour or an even number is $\frac{9}{13}$. In the same way, the sets $H \cup N = S$, so $n(H \cup N) = n(S) = 13$, and the probability of drawing an honour or a non-honour is $\frac{13}{13} = 1$. This event is called the *certain* event. On the other hand, $E \cap O = \varnothing$, so the probability of drawing an even *and* an odd number is zero—the *impossible* event.*

You can see that, once the probability model has been set up, elementary deductions from it are a simple matter. The real problem is the choice of the correct model. Bad shuffling may have put all the honours on the left of the table, and the person conducting the experiment may have an unconscious tendency to choose a card from the right of the table: in this case, it would not be reasonable to assign equal probabilities to each sample point, and then to deduce that the probability of drawing an honour is $\frac{5}{13}$. The usual way to get round this difficulty is to say that the probabilities of each sample point will be equal if a card is chosen "at random". When we inquire a little further, and ask what is meant by choosing a card at random, we come to the answer—in such a manner that the probabilities of each sample point are equal. This gets us nowhere. Probability theory, like all mathematics, is essentially abstract, and will only give us meaningful answers in real life if we choose a model which approximates very closely to the real-life situation. The *usefulness* of mathematics depends on the choice of the correct system to employ for the problem in hand.

---

* We may use the words "certain" and "impossible" here because we have confined our discussion to *finite* sample spaces. When dealing with *infinite* sample spaces, an event may be possible and yet have probability zero. Consider the sample space whose points are the positive real numbers less than 1. If each sample point is to be assigned the same probability, what should that probability be?

To return to our sample space $S$. Suppose now that the cards were placed into two boxes, one containing the honours, and the other containing the rest. A better model for this situation would be to say that the probability of event $H$ is now $1/2$, and since this will be the sum of the probabilities of the sample points in $H$, each of these five sample points should be assigned probability $\frac{1}{10}$. Similarly, the remaining sample points should be assigned probability $\frac{1}{16}$. Now consider the event $E$,

$$E = \{2, 4, 6, 8, 10\}$$

The first four of these members have probability $\frac{1}{16}$ and the last has probability $\frac{1}{10}$, so the probability of $E$ is $\frac{4}{16} + \frac{1}{10} = \frac{7}{20}$. On our previous model the probability of the same event $E$ was $\frac{5}{13}$. Both answers are correct, but correspond approximately to two different real-life situations.

### EXERCISE 2

1. The sample space $D = \{1, 2, 3, 4, 5, 6\}$ forms the basis of a probability model to investigate the rolling of a die. If all sample points are equally likely, find the probabilities of (a) 4; (b) an even number; (c) a prime number; (d) a multiple of three; (e) an even number *or* a prime; (f) an even number *and* a prime. (N.B. 1 is not generally accepted as a prime.)

2. The die is now loaded so that 6 appears three times as often as its opposite number, 1. The other numbers are equally likely, and will appear twice as often as 1. What probabilities should be assigned to the various sample points? Find the probabilities of the same events as in Q.1.

### Cartesian Products

Suppose a die is thrown and a coin tossed simultaneously. The coin shows heads and the die shows 3. This event can be written as the *ordered pair* $\{(H, 3)\}$. In the same way, the event that the coin shows tails and the die shows an odd number can be shown as the set of ordered pairs

$$\{(T, 1), (T, 3), (T, 5)\}$$

The pairs are called ordered because we are writing the result of the coin first and the result of the die second. If we consider the die on its own, the sample space is

$$D = \{1, 2, 3, 4, 5, 6\}$$

and for the coin on its own the sample space is

$$P = \{H, T\}$$

When we throw both coin and die, and consider the possible pairs, we have the sample space

$\{(H, 1), (H, 2), (H, 3), (H, 4), (H, 5), (H, 6), (T, 1), (T, 2), (T, 3), (T, 4),$
$\quad (T, 5), (T, 6)\}$

This set is called the *Cartesian product* of $P$ and $D$, and is denoted by the symbol

$$P \times D$$

This is a non-commutative operation, since the order of the letters $P$ and $D$ corresponds to the fact that the pairs in the product are written with the members of $P$ first and the members of $D$ second. Notice also that

$$n(P) = 2$$
$$n(D) = 6$$
$$\text{and } n(P \times D) = 2 \times 6 = 12.$$

If we assign probability $\frac{1}{2}$ to each point in $P$ and probability $\frac{1}{6}$ to each point in $D$, then each point in $P \times D$ is assigned probability $\frac{1}{12} (= \frac{1}{2} \times \frac{1}{6})$. If we throw two dice (or one die twice) our sample space will be the set

$$D \times D$$

and since $n(D) = 6$, we have $n(D \times D) = 6 \times 6 = 36$. The pairs of $D \times D$ are listed below:

$(1, 1), (1, 2), (1, 3), (1, 4), (1, 5), (1, 6),$
$(2, 1), (2, 2), (2, 3), (2, 4), (2, 5), (2, 6),$
$(3, 1), (3, 2), (3, 3), (3, 4), (3, 5), (3, 6),$
$(4, 1), (4, 2), (4, 3), (4, 4), (4, 5), (4, 6),$
$(5, 1), (5, 2), (5, 3), (5, 4), (5, 5), (5, 6),$
$(6, 1), (6, 2), (6, 3), (6, 4), (6, 5), (6, 6).$

If we assign to each simple event in this sample space the probability $\frac{1}{36}$, then we can find the probability that, for example, the sum of the numbers on the two dice is 10. If we denote this event by the letter $T$, then by examining the list we see that

$$T = \{(4, 6), (5, 5), (6, 4)\}$$

and so the probability of $T$ is $\frac{3}{36}$, or $\frac{1}{12}$.

## EXERCISE 3

**1.** Using the probability model just discussed, what is the probability of (a) the sum of the numbers on two dice being exactly 7; (b) the sum being 4 or less; (c) the product being 12; (d) the product being 32; (e) the sum being an even number; (f) the product being an odd number?

**2.** The sample space $D \times D$ would be equally appropriate if we took two piles of six cards, each numbered from 1 to 6, and drew one card from each pile. If, however, we had only one such pile of cards, drew a card, *put it aside*, and then drew another card, which members of $D \times D$ would now have the probability zero? What probability should be assigned to the remaining sample points? Using this probability model, answer the same questions as in Q.1, replacing the word "dice" by the word "cards".

**3.** $P = \{H, T\}$ is the sample space associated with the tossing of a single coin. The tossing of the same coin twice (or of two different coins) is represented by $P \times P$. List the members of $P \times P$. What is the probability of getting (a) two heads; (b) a head and a tail?

**4.** If three coins are tossed, the sample space is $P \times P \times P$. What is the value of $n(P \times P \times P)$? List the set. What is the probability of throwing (a) three heads; (b) two tails and a head?

**5.** What is $n(P \times P \times P \times P)$? List the set. What is the probability of throwing two heads and two tails with four coins?

**6.** Imagine you have three cardboard discs, numbered 1, 2 and 3. Each disc has one side marked $A$ and the other marked $B$. The experiment of taking a disc and placing it on the table might result in disc number 3 being taken and placed with side $A$ uppermost. This event we denote by the symbol $3A$. List the appropriate sample space for this experiment. Now assume that both sides of disc number 1 are coloured black, both sides of disc number 2 are coloured white, and that disc number 3 has side $A$ coloured black and side $B$ coloured white. What is the probability that, if a disc is drawn and placed on the table, (a) it has a black face uppermost and a black face below, and (b) it has a black face uppermost and a white face below? If the discs were coloured as described but not marked in any other way, and a friend laid one on the table in front of you, is it more likely that the hidden side is the same colour as the exposed side, or that it is a different colour?

## Dependent events

We return to the pile of six cards, numbered 1 to 6, which we mentioned in Q.2 of the last exercise. If a friend removes one card, and we then take one ourselves, what is the probability that we have drawn the 3? It rather depends on what we know about the card our friend has removed. The appropriate sample space is that listed as $D \times D$ on p. 37 with the pairs of equal numbers removed, so that the probability of each sample point is $\frac{1}{30}$. If we know nothing about our friend's card, we must count how many pairs have 3 as their *second* member. There are 5 such pairs, so that the probability of our drawing a 3 *if we know nothing about the card removed* is $\frac{5}{30} = \frac{1}{6}$. But suppose we know that our friend has *not* removed the 3: we denote this event (the 3 not removed) by $X$. Our sample space is now reduced by removing the five pairs which have 3 as their *first* member, so that the probability of each sample point is now $\frac{1}{25}$, and since the sample space still contains five pairs whose *second* member is 3, the probability of our drawing a 3 *if we know that the 3 has not been removed* is $\frac{1}{5}$. If we denote the event of our drawing the 3 as $Y$, this probability is known as *the probability of Y given X*, and is denoted by the symbol

$$P(Y|X).$$

If we denote by $Z$ the event that the 3 *has* been removed, then our sample space, given event $Z$, is reduced to

$$\{(3, 1), (3, 2), (3, 4), (3, 5), (3, 6)\}$$

None of the sample points has 3 as its second element, so the probability of our drawing the 3 is zero (as is otherwise obvious). Thus we have

$$P(Y) = \frac{1}{6}$$
$$P(Y|X) = \frac{1}{5}$$
$$P(Y|Z) = 0$$

The last two are called *conditional* probabilities, as they depend on the events $X$ and $Z$.

To clarify ideas, consider a sample space $S$ whose sample points are the positive integers from 1 to 12, that is

$$S = \{1, 2, 3, 4, 5, 6, 7, 8, 9, 10, 11, 12\}$$

and two sets $A$ and $B$, whose members are factors of 12 and 16 respectively, so that

$$A = \{1, 2, 3, 4, 6, 12\}$$
$$B = \{1, 2, 4, 8\}$$

We assign to each sample point in $S$ the same probability, namely $\frac{1}{12}$. Since $n(A) = 6$, the probability of $A$ is $\frac{6}{12}$, i.e.

$$P(A) = \frac{1}{2}$$

If now event $B$ is given, then event $A$ can only occur in the cases where an element of $A$ is also an element of $B$. In other words, the sample space has been reduced to $B$, and the event $A$ has been reduced to the event $A \cap B$. Since $n(A \cap B) = 3$ and $n(B) = 4$, we have

$$P(A \mid B) = \tfrac{3}{4}$$

Notice that this probability can be written as $\frac{3/12}{4/12}$, which is the probability of $A \cap B$ in the *original* sample space divided by the probability of $B$ in the original sample space. In general, if $A$ and $B$ are events in a sample space $S$, then $P(A \mid B) = \dfrac{P(A \cap B)}{P(B)}$ (assuming $P(B) \neq 0$), the probabilities on the right being calculated in $S$.

This formula can be rewritten as

$$P(A \cap B) = P(B).P(A \mid B)$$

a form we shall find useful later.

Two events are said to be independent if the probability of either is not affected by the knowledge that the other has occurred. Symbolically, if we have two events $A$ and $B$, and we calculate $P(A)$ and $P(A \mid B)$, and these have the same value, then we say that $A$ is independent of $B$. We can write the *condition* that $A$ is independent of $B$ in the form

$$P(A) = P(A \mid B).$$

If we combine this with the formula above, we reach the conclusion that if $A$ is independent of $B$, then

$$P(A \cap B) = P(A).P(B).$$

The symmetry of this formula tells us that if $A$ is independent of $B$, then $B$ is independent of $A$.

As an example, suppose we toss two coins and use the sample space

$$\{(h, h), (h, t), (t, h), (t, t)\}$$

where each sample point has probability $1/4$. Now let $A$ be the event that at least one head has appeared:

$$A = \{(h, h), (h, t), (t, h)\}$$

similarly, let $B$ be the event that at least one tail has appeared:

$$B = \{(h, t), (t, h), (t, t)\}$$

Then we have $A \cap B = \{(h, t), (t, h)\}$

Now $$P(A) = 3/4$$
$$P(B) = 3/4$$
$$P(A \cap B) = 1/2$$

so that the two numbers $P(A \cap B)$ and $P(A).P(B)$ are $1/2$ and $9/16$ respectively. Since these numbers are not equal, the two events are not independent. The knowledge that at least one tail has appeared affects the probability that at least one head will have appeared, and vice versa.

### EXERCISE 4

1. Two coins are thrown, and events $Y$ and $Z$ are defined as follows:

   $Y$: the two faces on view are not the same:

   $Z$: at least one tail is on view.

Are $Y$ and $Z$ independent?

2. Three coins are thrown, and events $Y$ and $Z$ are defined as follows:

   $Y$: the three faces on view are not all the same:

   $Z$: at least one tail is on view.

Are $Y$ and $Z$ independent?

3. Two dice are rolled, and events $A$ and $B$ are defined as follows:

   $A$: the first die shows 6.

   $B$: the second die shows an odd number.

*Assuming* that these events are independent, what is the probability of the event $A \cap B$?

4. In order to achieve a "double", a punter has to name the winner of two races. Assuming that the events are independent, and that the probabilities of his naming the first and second winners are $1/8$ and $2/13$ respectively, what is the probability of his achieving the double?

### Bayes' Theorem

A market-research firm investigating on behalf of the makers of "Coffin" cigarettes comes up with the following facts:

Of the cigarette-smoking population, 70% are men and 30% are women.

10% of these men and 20% of these women smoke "Coffins".

Problem: what is the probability that a person seen smoking a "Coffin" will be a man?

Our sample space is the set of all cigarette smokers, and we shall use the symbols $M$, $W$ and $C$ to denote the sets of men, women and "Coffin" smokers respectively. Now we have

$$P(M) = 7/10$$
$$P(W) = 3/10$$
$$P(C\,|\,M) = 1/10$$
$$P(C\,|\,W) = 1/5$$

Notice that $M \cap W = \varnothing$ and $M \cup W =$ the whole sample space, that is, the whole sample space is partitioned into two disjoint sets. Similarly, the set $C$ is partitioned into two disjoint sets $C \cap M$ and $C \cap W$. The whole situation can be seen diagrammatically as follows:

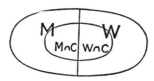

The whole diagram represents the sample space, divided into the sets $M$ and $W$, and the inner oval represents the set $C$. We have at once

$$P(C) = P(M \cap C) + P(W \cap C)$$

Now $P(M \cap C) = P(M) . P(C\,|\,M) = 7/10 \times 1/10 = 7/100$
and similarly $P(W \cap C) = 3/50$,
so that $P(C) = 7/100 + 3/50 = 13/100$.
We are trying to calculate $P(M\,|\,C)$, which is given by the definition

$$P(M\,|\,C) = \frac{P(M \cap C)}{P(C)}$$

$$= \frac{7/100}{13/100}$$

$$= \frac{7}{13}$$

Thus the probability of a person smoking a "Coffin" being a man is 7/13. Examine carefully the various steps in this argument. In full, we have

$$P(M\,|\,C) = \frac{\frac{7}{10} \times \frac{1}{10}}{(\frac{7}{10} \times \frac{1}{10}) + (\frac{3}{10} \times \frac{1}{5})}$$

or, speaking generally,

$$P(M\,|\,C) = \frac{P(M) . P(C\,|\,M)}{P(M) . P(C\,|\,M) + P(W) . P(C\,|\,W)}$$

This is a special case of Bayes' Theorem, which can be extended to cases with more subdivisions than the one discussed by adding further terms to the denominator on the right-hand side: we have of course proved nothing here: the formula above is no more than a mental jump from the consideration of a special case.

### EXERCISE 5

1. Given a sample space $S$ and two subsets $A$ and $B$ such that $A \cup B = S$ and $A \cap B = \emptyset$, together with an event $E$, prove that

$$P(A \mid E) = \frac{P(A).P(E \mid A)}{P(A).P(E/A) + P(B).P(E \mid B)}$$

2. In a certain hospital 40% of cases were discharged within a week. Of those so discharged, 25% had been admitted with broken bones, whilst of those not discharged within a week 10% had been admitted with broken bones. If you were admitted with a broken bone, what is the probability that you will be discharged within a week? ("Other things being equal").

## CHAPTER IV

# More Relations

In Volume 1 a relation was defined as a set of ordered pairs. Given any two sets $A$ and $B$ the Cartesian product of $A$ and $B$ is the set of all possible pairs whose first elements are members of $A$ and whose second elements are members of $B$. In symbols,

$$A \times B = \{(x, y): x \in A, y \in B\}$$

Any subset of this product is a relation, whose domain is a subset of $A$ and whose range is a subset of $B$. In many cases (but not all) the relation in $A \times B$ is defined by some property, that is, $y$ is related to $x$ in some way. Examples of such properties are

$y$ is the sister of $x$
$y = 2x$
$y$ is a subset of $x$
$y$ divides $x$.

When we talk of relations generally it is useful to have some notation to describe a property without stating any particular property: for this we shall write

$$yRx$$

meaning "$y$ is related to $x$ (in some way, but we are not concerned with details)".

To take a particular example, suppose

$$A = \{2, 3, 4\}$$
$$B = \{5, 6, 7, 8\}$$

then $A \times B$ contains 12 pairs,

(2, 5), (2, 6), (2, 7), (2, 8),
(3, 5), (3, 6), (3, 7), (3, 8),
(4, 5), (4, 6), (4, 7), (4, 8).

Suppose further that $yRx$ is to mean the property

$y$ is an integral multiple of $x$

which can be expressed very simply in the form

$$y/x \in Z$$

(where $Z$ stands for the set of all integers).
We can write the relation in symbols as

$$\{(x, y): x \in A, y \in B, y/x \in Z\}$$

This relation only contains four pairs,

$$\{(2, 6), (2, 8), (3, 6), (4, 8)\}$$

Such a relation can be illustrated graphically. The diagram shows the whole set $A \times B$, with the members of the relation just discussed marked by small circles:

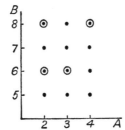

Another graphical illustration is given in this diagram:

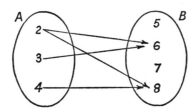

Here the set $A$ (from which the first elements are drawn) is shown on the left, and the set $B$ on the right. Arrows run from the first elements to the corresponding second elements. Notice that every member of $A$ appears in the relation, so that $A$ is itself the domain, but only the elements $\{6, 8\}$ of B actually appear in the relation itself (they are the only members of $B$ "with arrows attached") so that this, and not $B$ itself, forms the range.

If the arrows in the second diagram were reversed, we should have another relation in which members of $B$ formed the first elements and members of $A$ the second elements. This is called the *inverse* of the original relation, and we would write

$$xR^{-1}y$$

If $R$ means "is an integral multiple of"
then $R^{-1}$ means "is an integral divisor of".
Finally, we remark that in the diagram, it is possible for more than one arrow to arrive at an element of $B$, and more than one arrow to leave an element of $A$. For this reason the relation is called a many-to-many relation.

The next diagram illustrates a relation between a set $C$ of children and a set $H$ of houses in a street. In symbols, the relation is

$$\{(x, y): x \in C, y \in H, x \text{ lives at } y\}$$

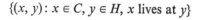

Here again it is possible for more than one arrow to arrive at an element of $H$, but it is *not* possible for more than one arrow to leave an element of $C$. This is a many-to-one relation, or *function*. The essential property of a function is that if we choose a first element, we are led *without doubt* to a *unique* second element, whatever our initial choice. This was not true in the previous example, where the choice of the number 2 would have left us in doubt whether to proceed to 6 or to 8.

A function is often called a *mapping*: we say that the property or rule maps the set $C$ into the set $H$. Another way of representing the above function diagrammatically would be as follows:

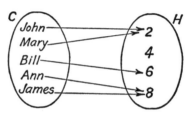

The idea of a function or mapping is a very wide one, and is not confined to finite sets. If we take the set of all real numbers, $R$, we can define a function in $R \times R$ which maps every member of $R$ into another member of $R$. A simple example is the function

$$\{(x, y): x, y \in R, y = 2x\}$$

We can choose any real number $x$ whatever, and the rule leaves us in no doubt where to proceed from there. If we choose $x = 3$, then the rule takes us to $y = 6$, and so on. A geometrical example is afforded by the following diagram:

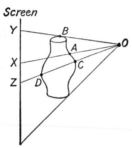

The "rule" is to imagine a ray of light leaving the point $O$ and casting a shadow of the object shown on the screen on the left. Thus $A$ maps into $X$, $B$ maps into $Y$, both $C$ and $D$ map into $Z$, and so on. Every point of the object will map into its unique image, though of course it is possible for two points to share the same image.

### EXERCISE 1

1. Take a piece of graph paper and a set of coordinate axes. Mark the points $(1, 1)$, $(2, 1)$, $(3, 1)$, $(2, 2)$, $(2, 0)$, $(2, -1)$. Now consider the function that maps each of these points into its reflection in the $x$ axis. Mark the image of each given point on the same diagram as you have marked the original points.

2. Using the same points as specified in Q.1, consider the function that maps each point into a point twice as far from the origin. Mark the image of each point as in Q.1.

3. Again starting with the same set of points, illustrate as before the function that maps each point $(x, y)$ into a point $(p, q)$ such that

$$p = x + y$$
$$q = x - y$$

4. Repeat Q.3 using the function

$$p = 3x - y$$
$$q = 6x - 2y$$

5. Repeat Q.3 using the function

$$p = x^2 - y^2$$
$$q = 2xy$$

## Equivalence Relations

We return for a moment to the function on p. 46 relating a set of children to the set of houses in a street. Instead of thus relating two different sets, we now specify a relation between the set $C$ and itself:

$$E = \{(x, y): x, y \in C, y \text{ lives in the same house as } x\}$$

Let us list the pairs of this relation:

- (a) (John, Mary)
- (b) (Mary, John)
- (c) (John, John)
- (d) (Mary, Mary)
- (e) (Bill, Bill)
- (f) (Ann, James)
- (g) (James, Ann)
- (h) (Ann, Ann)
- (j) (James, James)

There are several points to note. Since we are dealing in ordered pairs, (a) and (b) are different, but are nevertheless both members of the relation. Similarly for (f) and (g). (c) looks a little odd, but after all John does live in the same house as himself, and we have never objected to plotting points like (2, 2) on a graph. This last property clearly applies to every member of the set $C$: each one lives in the same house as himself. In symbols,

$$xRx$$

where $R$ stands for the property "lives in the same house as" and $x$ stands for any member of the set $C$. A relation which has this property for every member of a set $S$ is called *reflexive*.

The other property of this relation already mentioned is that if, say, (John, Mary) is a member, then so is (Mary, John). If any pair $(x, y)$ is a member, then so is $(y, x)$. This may be written

$$xRy \Leftrightarrow yRx$$

A relation with this property is called *symmetric*. The relation we are discussing is both reflexive and symmetric.

Suppose now that John has a brother Charles who lives in the same house with him and Mary. The set $C$ has now been extended, but not otherwise altered. However, the relation $E$ will now contain the following extra pairs:

(k) (John, Charles)
(l) (Charles, John)
(m) (Mary, Charles)
(n) (Charles, Mary)
(o) (Charles, Charles)

Clearly there is a connection between the original pair (b) and the two new pairs (n) and (l). If John lives in the same house as Mary, and Mary lives in the same house as Charles, then John lives in the same house as Charles. If (John)$R$(Mary) *and* (Mary)$R$(Charles) then (John)$R$(Charles): in general

$$xRy \text{ and } yRz \Rightarrow xRz$$

A relation with this property is called *transitive*. The relation $E$ in the extended set $C$ just discussed has all the three properties we have mentioned: because of this, it is called an *equivalence relation*. It divides the extended set $C$ into three subsets,

{John, Mary, Charles}
{Bill}
{Ann, James}

Each member of a given subset shares with the other members of the subset the common property that they all live in the same house. Every member of the original set is accounted for, every subset contains at least one member, and there is no overlapping, that is, the subsets are disjoint. The original set has been *partitioned* into non-empty, disjoint subsets which between them exhaust the original set.

To sum up, a relation with defining property $R$ in a set $S$ is called an equivalence relation if for all $x, y, z \in S$,

(1) $xRx$        (reflexive)
(2) $xRy \Leftrightarrow yRx$        (symmetric)
(3) $xRy \text{ and } yRz \Rightarrow xRz$        (transitive)

EXERCISE 2

1. Consider the following relations:

(a) the relation "sits next to" on the set of pupils in your classroom:
(b) the relation "is taller than" on the same set:

(c) the relation "is equal to" on the set of integers:

(d) the relation "is congruent to" on the set of plane polygons:

(e) the relation "is parallel to" on the set of all lines in a given plane:

(f) the relation "has the same area as" on the set of plane figures:

(g) the relation "leaves the same remainder on division by 5" on the set of positive integers:

(h) the relation "is an integral divisor of" on the set of positive integers:

(i) the relation "is a subset of" on the set of all subsets of $\{a, b, c\}$

List those relations which are (i) symmetric, (ii) reflexive, (iii) transitive. Which of these relations are equivalence relations?

## The rational numbers

In Volume 1 it was pointed out that the word "number" is rather imprecise. We should always be clear whether we are speaking of the positive integers $(Z^+)$, the integers $(Z)$, the rational numbers $(Q)$ or the real numbers $(R)$. Furthermore we have assumed that we knew the properties of these various sets of numbers without much investigation. The fact that $\sqrt{2} \times \sqrt{2} = 2$ is a matter of definition, but can we be sure that $\sqrt{2} \times \sqrt{8} = 4$? And in any case, what do we mean by the number 2? We may be convinced that $1 + 1 = 2$, but in Chapter I we saw that it is perfectly correct to write in certain circumstances that $1 + 1 = 1$. A full discussion of these matters is well outside our scope, but such problems have exercised mathematicians for a long time.

We start, then, by *assuming* certain familiar properties of the integers, $Z$. To clarify our ideas, we shall list them here, starting with some properties of *addition*.

1. If we add any two integers, the result is another integer. For example, $(-3) + (+7) = (+4)$. This property is known as *closure*. We say that the integers are *closed under addition*.

2. For any three integers $a$, $b$, $c$,

$$(a+b) + c = a + (b+c).$$

That is, we can pair the integers as we like when adding three of them together. This is the *associative* property.

3. There is an *identity element*, the number 0, with the property that for any integer $a$,

$$a + 0 = a.$$

An identity element is one which, when combined with any other element, leaves it unchanged.

4. Every integer $a$ has an *inverse*, $a'$, such that

$$a + a' = 0 \text{ (the identity element)}.$$

For example, the inverse of $(+4)$ is $(-4)$, since

$$(+4) + (-4) = 0.$$

The above four properties of the integers ensure that the integers form a *group** under addition. There is the additional property

5. For any two integers, $a + b = b + a$. This is the *commutative* property. A group with this property is called a *commutative group.*

Now let us see if the operation of multiplication has the same properties when applied to the integers:

1. *Closure.* Yes. The product of two integers is always another integer.

2. *Associative property.* Yes. $(a \times b) \times c = a \times (b \times c)$ for all integers $a$, $b$ and $c$.

3. *Identity element.* Yes. The integer 1 will serve.

$$a \times 1 = a \text{ for every integer } a.$$

4. *Inverses.* No. $a$ and $a'$ will be inverses if and only if $a \times a' = 1$. There is clearly no *integer* $a'$ such that, for example, $5 \times a' = 1$.

5. *Commutative property.* Yes. $a \times b = b \times a$ for all integers. Because of the breakdown in Property 4, the intergers do *not* form a group under multiplication. It was to get round this weakness that fractions were invented (though of course the first people to use fractions had never heard of a group in this formal sense!). If we allow fractions, then $5 \times \frac{1}{5} = 1$, and 5 has an inverse. But—is 5 a fraction? And what about 0? Has it an inverse? Do the fractions have the other properties of a group under addition and under multiplication? It is to tidy up our ideas on these points that we discuss the system of rational numbers.

We started our analysis of the integers by assuming that we knew what they were. In discussing rational numbers, however, we shall *define* a rational number in terms of these same integers, and we shall *define* what we mean by the addition and multiplication of such numbers, *assuming* that we know what we mean by these operations when applied to integers.

* For a further discussion of groups see Matthews, *Matrices 2.*

A *rational number*, then, is an ordered pair of integers $(p, q)$ where $q$ is *not* 0.

*Multiplication* is defined by the following formula:

$$(p, q) \times (r, s) = (pr, qs).$$

Does this satisfy the closure property? Since $p$, $q$, $r$, $s$ are all integers, $pr$ and $qs$ are also integers, but suppose $qs = 0$? The second element must not be zero, or the pair would not satisfy the definition of a rational number. In fact, since $q$ and $s$ are both non-zero, we "know" that $qs$ is not zero, but here we are appealing to a property of the integers which we have not yet mentioned, and which we ought to have either listed or proved. We cannot prove it from the properties listed so far, and therefore we must admit that we are going to take this as an assumption.* In this case, we have the desired closure, and it is not difficult to see that the associative property holds and that the rational number $(1, 1)$ will serve as an identity element. The commutative property also holds, but what about inverses? We may argue that $(p, q)$ is just another way of writing $\frac{p}{q}$, and that our multiplication definition just tells us that

$$\frac{p}{q} \times \frac{r}{s} = \frac{pr}{qs}$$

In this case the inverse of say $\frac{3}{8}$ is obviously $\frac{8}{3}$, since

$$\tfrac{3}{8} \times \tfrac{8}{3} = 1.$$

But according to our definition, $(3, 8) \times (8, 3) = (24, 24)$, and we have given no reason why $(24, 24)$ should be the same as $(1, 1)$. This means another diversion: in order to settle the matter of inverses, we must re-define the sign "$=$" in such a way that it *will* be logically true to say that $(24, 24) = (1, 1)$. You will now see how difficult it is to try to put even such a simple idea as a fraction on a sound logical basis.

EXERCISE 3

1. This is part of a multiplication table in which the product

| | 1 | 2 | 3 | 4 |
|---|---|---|---|---|
| 1 | | | | |
| 2 | 2 | 4 | 1 | 3 |
| 3 | 3 | 1 | 4 | 2 |
| 4 | | | | |

* See also p. 54.

is obtained by first performing ordinary multiplication and then subtracting 5, 10 or 15 if necessary in order to reduce the answer to a number less than 5. Complete the table and check whether each of the four group properties holds. (Compare with the patterns on the covers of this book: could you match one of them exactly by a slight alteration of the order of the rows and columns?)

2. Do the odd integers form a group under addition?
3. Do the even integers form a group under addition?
4. See *Matrices 1*, p. 65. Is this an example of a group?

### Rational numbers and equivalence classes

If we take two "fractions" which look different but are "equal", we see that they can lead us to a definition of equality for rational numbers. For example, the two fractions $\frac{3}{4}$ and $\frac{9}{12}$, which are "equal", have the "cross-multiplying" property that $3 \times 12 = 4 \times 9$. Using this idea, we define a relation $R$ on the set of rational numbers so that for any two rationals $a = (p, q)$, $b = (r, s)$,

$$aRb \Leftrightarrow ps = qr.$$

If $a = (p, q), b = (r, s), c = (t, u)$
We have $aRb \Leftrightarrow ps = qr$
$bRc \Leftrightarrow ru = st$.
If $aRb$ and $bRc$, then $psru = qrst$,

$$\Leftrightarrow (pu)(rs) = (qt)(rs) \text{ (using properties (2) and (5))}.$$

Now by cancellation we have $pu = qt$, leading to $aRc$, and the fact that the relation is transitive. But is cancellation valid? We have not listed it as a property of the integers: here is another gap in our foundations, which we repair by another assumption:

$$ab = ac \text{ and } a \neq 0 \Rightarrow b = c.*$$

By inserting this assumption, we have been able to show that this relation $R$ is transitive. You should now show for yourself that it is both reflexive and symmetric, and thus that it is an equivalence relation.

We have seen (informally) on p. 49 that an equivalence relation such as this will divide the set of rationals into an exhaustive set of disjoint subsets: one such subset is

$$\{(2, 3), (4, 6), (6, 9), (9, 12), \ldots\}$$

* We can prove this from the earlier assumption on p. 52 that the product of two non-zero numbers is non-zero.

and another is

$$\{(3, 1), (6, 2), (9, 3), \ldots\}$$

Each of these is called an *equivalence class*, and we *define* equality of rational numbers by saying that two such numbers are equal if they are members of the same equivalence class as specified by the relation just discussed. Indeed, we might have defined a rational number as an equivalence class in the first place, and formal works on this topic frequently do so. In order to prop up our argument we have had recourse to various assumptions as we went along, which in a formal approach would have been better stated at the beginning. There is in fact one other assumption which we have not mentioned, but which is commonly accepted as a basic property of the integers: it is the *distributive* property

$$a(b + c) = ab + ac$$

which links addition and multiplication. The full list of assumptions (or axioms) then looks like this:

|  | Multiplication | Addition |
|---|---|---|
| *Closure* | Yes | Yes |
| *Associative* | Yes | Yes |
| *Identity element* | Yes   (1) | Yes   (0) |
| *Inverses* | No | Yes |
| *Cancellation* | Yes (except by 0) | (Yes, but it can be proved from the other axioms) |
| *Distributive property* | Yes, for multiplication over addition | |

These are the axioms for the integers. From them, we can in fact deduce other assumptions that we have made, such as the statement on p. 52 that if $a \neq 0$, $b \neq 0$, then $ab \neq 0$. Using these axioms and our definition of rational numbers and the equality of rational numbers, we can prove that they have all the properties listed for integers, and that they also have inverses for multiplication (except that (0, 1) has no inverse). To do this we must define multiplication, which we have done, and also addition, which is done as follows:

$$(p, q) + (r, s) = (ps + qr, qs).$$

Because the rationals satisfy the properties listed *and* have inverses for multiplication, they are said to form a *field*.

### Exercise 4

1. Why, do you think, is the addition of rationals defined as shown?

2. Using this definition, try to prove the associative property of addition and the distributive property.

3. Try to deduce from the axioms for integers listed on p. 54 the *theorem* that $a.0 = 0$. (You may regard this as obvious, but it is not a listed axiom, and so we should be able to prove it from the axioms.)

4. Try to deduce from the given axioms for integers and the theorem that $a.0 = 0$ the further theorem that if $a \neq 0$ and $b \neq 0$, then $ab \neq 0$.

## Order Relations

Another basic property of the integers which we normally assume without discussion is that they form an *ordered* set. Two given numbers are either equal or one is greater than the other. A common symbol which we have already met to describe this relation is the symbol

which we interpret as meaning

"less than or equal to".

This symbol has four basic properties when applied to numbers which we accept without question: they are

1. $a \leqslant a$.

This means that the relation holds between any number and itself, and is therefore reflexive. We have already seen that an equivalence relation also has this property.

2. If $a \leqslant b$ and $b \leqslant a$, then $a = b$. Contrast this with the symmetric property of an equivalence relation. There we had that if $aRb$, then $bRa$ always: here this is only true if $a = b$. For this reason the property listed is known as the *anti-symmetric* property.

3. If $a \leqslant b$ and $b \leqslant c$, then $a \leqslant c$. This is the same transitive property as is possessed by equivalence relations.

4. For all $a$, $b$, either $a \leqslant b$ or $b \leqslant a$. This property means that *every* $a$ and $b$ are related by the symbol $\leqslant$.

Any relation between the members of a set which has the four properties listed above is said to be a *total ordering*.

### EXERCISE 5

1. List all the eight subsets of the set $\{a, b, c\}$. Give examples to show that these subsets may be related by the symbol $\subset$ (with its usual meaning) and that this relation satisfies the first three properties of a total ordering as listed above. Give also an example to show that property 4 does *not* hold. Such a relation is called a *partial ordering*.

2. The following family tree shows the descendants of one man, together with their dates of birth:

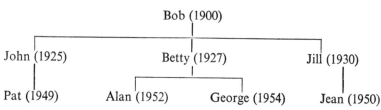

Bob (1900)

John (1925)        Betty (1927)        Jill (1930)

Pat (1949)     Alan (1952)     George (1954)     Jean (1950)

State whether any of the following relations are equivalence relations or order relations on this set, and in the case of order relations state whether the ordering is total or partial.

     (a) is not older than
     (b) is a member of a later generation than
     (c) is a member of the same generation as
     (d) is a child of
     (e) is a descendant of

### One-to-one correspondence

If $P$ is the set of pupils present in a class and $D$ is the set of occupied desks in that classroom, then there is (usually) a one-to-one correspondence between the sets $P$ and $D$, defined by the relation

$$\{(d, p): d \in D, p \in P, p \text{ is sitting at } d\}$$

Normally every pupil is sitting at only one desk, and every desk contains only one pupil. We take it as obvious that in these circumstances there are as many pupils as occupied desks: in fact, if the teacher knows that the room contains 32 desks, and that *every* desk is occupied by exactly one pupil, then he need not count the number of pupils to check for absentees—he knows that there must be 32 pupils present.

The process of counting is simply setting up a one-to-one correspondence between the set of objects being counted and a subset of the positive integers. A very small child asked how many dolls she has might

say "there's Betty, that's one, Joan, that's two, Mary, that's three—
I've got three". Each doll has been assigned just one number, and each
number of the set $\{1, 2, 3\}$ has been assigned to just one doll. By using
the fact that $\{1, 2, 3\}$ is an *ordered* set, she has arrived at the conclusion
that she has three dolls. We can *define* counting by saying that two sets
have the same number of members if and only if it is possible to find a
one-to-one correspondence between them.

This may seem to be using a sledgehammer to crack a nut, but a
mathematician likes to frame his definitions from a consideration of the
"obvious", and then to make his deductions from these definitions: it
may well be that his deductions are by no means obvious—indeed, they
may be almost incredible. We take this definition of what we mean by
saying that two sets have the same number of elements, then, and consider the two *infinite* sets

$$A = \{1, 2, 3, 4, 5, 6, 7, \ldots\}$$
$$B = \{2, 4, 6, 8, 10, 12, 14, \ldots\}$$

It is certainly possible to find a one-to-one correspondence between
them: if we select any member of $A$, such as 4, then we can take as its
corresponding element in $B$ the number 8, which is twice 4: symbolically, we may consider the relation

$$\{(a, b): b \in B, a \in A, b=2a\}$$

Given any $a$, the corresponding $b$ is determined uniquely, and given
any $b$, the corresponding $a$ is determined uniquely: this is a one-to-one
correspondence, and hence *by definition* $A$ and $B$ contain the same number of elements. But every member of $B$ is also a member of $A$, although
the converse is not true: we say that $B$ is a *proper* subset of $A$. Speaking
informally, we have taken a set $A$ (in fact, our familiar positive integers,
$Z^+$), left out half of them (the odd numbers), and have then proved
that the set left, $B$, has as many members as the original set $A$. A sur-
prising result, but a logical consequence of our definition of the number
of elements in a set, which we were hardly prepared to quarrel with. If
we object to the result, we must frame a new definition which will lead
to a more acceptable result. In fact, no other suitable definition has
been found, so mathematicians are prepared to put up with this and
other strange consequences. They serve at least as a warning that infinite sets have peculiar properties, and that we must not too hastily
assume that rules which apply to finite sets can also be applied to
them.

## Exercise 6

1. Draw two parallel line-segments $AB$ and $CD$ of unequal length, join $AC$ and $BD$ and produce if necessary to meet at $O$. Now define a mapping from the points $P$ of the line $AB$ onto the points $Q$ of the line $CD$ as follows: choose $P$, join $OP$ and produce if necessary to meet $CD$ at $Q$: then $Q$ is the image of $P$. Is this in fact a mapping (function)? That is, can any $P$ produce two different possible points $Q$? Is it also a one-to-one correspondence? That is, can any $Q$ arise from two different points $P$? If it is a one-to-one correspondence, the number of elements in the two sets must be the same, i.e., there are as many points on the line-segment $AB$ as there are on $CD$.

2. The positive rational numbers $Q^+$ can be defined as the set of ordered pairs of numbers $p/q$ where $p$ and $q$ are positive integers ($p, q \in Z^+$). The subset of these numbers defined by the relation $p + q = 4$ contains

$$\tfrac{3}{1}, \ \tfrac{1}{3}, \ \tfrac{2}{2}.$$

We can place these three numbers in an *order* defined by the natural order of the numerators (1, 2, 3), thus:

$$\tfrac{1}{3}, \ \tfrac{2}{2}, \ \tfrac{3}{1}.$$

By taking a series of similar subsets of $Q^+$, starting with $p + q = 2$, then $p + q = 3$, then $p + q = 4$, etc., we can write down the members of $Q^+$ in a definite order (will this order be the same as the "natural" order of size of the fractions in the elementary sense?). Write down the first 15 members of this ordered set, and above the rational numbers write the positive integers in order. Does this set up a one-to-one correspondence between $Z^+$ and $Q^+$? What rational number corresponds to 13? What positive integer corresponds to 3/1? Must we conclude that the sets $Z^+$ and $Q^+$ contain the same number of members?

3. Try to set up a one-to-one correspondence between $Z^+$ and the set of positive *real* numbers $R^+$. If you fail, refer to the chapter called "Beyond the Googol" in the book *Mathematics and the Imagination* (Kasner and Newman).

## CHAPTER V

# Logic

## Propositions

We have already met the use of letters as symbols in many different ways. Letters have been used to represent numbers, operations, sets, states of switches, points, lines and people: even this list is not exhaustive. In this chapter we shall use letters to represent statements or propositions. For example, the proposition "I have had lunch" may be represented by the symbol $a$, and the proposition "I have had tea" by the symbol $b$. If it is early afternoon, it is likely that $a$ is a true proposition and $b$ a false one (assuming that we are talking about today's meals —we must, as always, be clear what we *are* talking about). If such is the case, we write

$$a = 1$$
$$b = 0.$$

Here is another use of the symbols 1 and 0: they are now associated with the truth or falsity of propositions, and, as in their use in switching algebra, there are no half-measures: we cannot in this context usefully discuss statements that are partly true, or which are a matter of opinion, such as the statement "this is a good painting" applied to some exhibit at the Royal Academy. Such a statement would not be called a proposition: a sentence is not a proposition unless it permits a definite decision as to whether it is true or false.

EXERCISE 1

Which of the following are propositions?

1. It is cloudy today.
2. John is fifteen years old.
3. 4 is an integer.
4. 6 is greater than 7.

5. $y$ is greater than 7 (assuming that someone will tell you what number $y$ represents).

6. Can you swim?

7. Get out of my sight.

### Compound Propositions

If I make the statement "I have had lunch and tea" I am in fact stating a compound proposition, containing two simple propositions

    *a*  I have had lunch
    *b*  I have had tea

and I am asserting that *both* are true: if I have missed either or both meals, then the compound proposition is not true. Using the letter $p$ to represent this compound proposition, we can exhibit this fact in a *truth table*,

| $a$ | $b$ | $p$ |
|-----|-----|-----|
| 0 | 0 | 0 |
| 0 | 1 | 0 |
| 1 | 0 | 0 |
| 1 | 1 | 1 |

Evidently this table is identical with the common multiplication table for the numbers 0 and 1, and also with the table for a circuit with two switches in series. For this reason, we write

$$p = ab.$$

This combination of propositions is called *conjunction*: it asserts *both a and b*. Another possible combination, called *disjunction*, asserts *either a or b (or both)*. If I return home from visiting friends, and to the question "have you had lunch or tea?" reply "yes", I am asserting that I have had at least one of these meals, and possibly both. The compound proposition ($q$) here would be false if and only if both $a$ and $b$ were false, and so the truth table looks like this:

| $a$ | $b$ | $q$ |
|-----|-----|-----|
| 0 | 0 | 0 |
| 0 | 1 | 1 |
| 1 | 0 | 1 |
| 1 | 1 | 1 |

Again you will see that this table is identical with that for the state of a circuit with two switches in parallel, and hence we shall write

$$q = a + b.$$

Notice the close relationship between the two methods of combination mentioned and the words "and" and "or".

*ab* may be read as "*a* and *b*":

*a* + *b* may be read as "*a* or *b*" (but this use of the word "or" does not exclude the possibility of both *a* and *b* being asserted: the remark "he is either a fool or a knave" admits the possibility that he is both a fool and a knave, and this is the meaning we attach to the word "or" here).

To complete the identification of our algebra of propositions with the algebra of circuits we define the *negation* of a proposition. The negation of *a* is the proposition "I have not had lunch", and the symbol we use for it is naturally $a'$. Clearly if $a = 0$ then $a' = 1$, and vice versa. If to the question "have you had lunch or tea?" I reply "no" then I am asserting the compound proposition $(a + b)'$. This is equivalent to the *conjunction* of the two propositions

I have not had lunch

*and*

I have not had tea

which can be written

$$a'b'$$

Thus we see that

$$(a + b)' = a'b'$$

where the "=" symbol here means, roughly, that the two compound propositions amount to the same thing, or, more precisely, that they have the same truth values for all given truth values of *a* and *b*.

EXERCISE 2

If $s = $ (I should like to go swimming today)

$t = $ (I should like to play tennis today)

write the following in reasonable and accurate English:

(1) $t'$  (2) $s + t$  (3) $st$  (4) $(st)'$  (5) $s't$  (6) $s't + st'$

## Implication

We have already used the symbol "$\Rightarrow$" and we have generally translated it by the word "implies". A more idiomatic translation is the form of words. if..., then...: thus

$$x \Rightarrow y$$

may be translated as

$$\text{if } x, \text{ then } y$$

Many a harassed mother with a small child, driven to bribery, has been heard to say "if you are a good boy, I shall buy you an ice cream". Here we have

$$x = \text{(you are a good boy)}$$
$$y = \text{(I shall buy you an ice cream)}$$

and we denote the compound proposition $x \Rightarrow y$ by the letter $c$. Now if the child is good and he gets his ice cream, his mother has stood by her promise: her remark is true. If, however, after being good, the boy does not get his ice cream, then his mother has made a false statement: $c = 0$. Thus two rows of the truth table can be completed:

| $x$ | $y$ | $c$ |
|-----|-----|-----|
| 1 | 1 | 1 |
| 1 | 0 | 0 |

If the boy is ill-behaved, and doesn't get his reward, he has nothing to complain of: his mother's statement was still true:

| $x$ | $y$ | $c$ |
|-----|-----|-----|
| 0 | 0 | 1 |

but small boys are cunning: his mother didn't say he wouldn't get an ice cream if he were naughty: she could still give him one without breaking her promise (and usually she gives in)

| $x$ | $y$ | $c$ |
|-----|-----|-----|
| 0 | 1 | 1 |

So the complete table for $c = (x \Rightarrow y)$ looks like this:

| $x$ | $y$ | $c$ |
|-----|-----|-----|
| 0 | 0 | 1 |
| 0 | 1 | 1 |
| 1 | 0 | 0 |
| 1 | 1 | 1 |

$c$ is only false when $x = 1$ and $y = 0$: in all other cases $c$ is true.

1. $p =$ (the polygon I have drawn is a triangle)
   $q =$ (the polygon I have drawn has two equal sides)
   $r =$ (the polygon I have drawn has two equal angles)

Write in reasonable and accurate English the proposition

$$(pq) \Rightarrow r.$$

Complete the following truth table:

| $p$ | $q$ | $r$ | $(pq)$ | $(pq) \Rightarrow r$ |
|-----|-----|-----|--------|----------------------|
| 0 | 0 | 0 | 0 | 1 |
| 0 | 0 | 1 | 0 | 1 |
| 0 | 1 | 0 | 0 | |
| 0 | 1 | 1 | 0 | |
| 1 | 0 | 0 | | |
| 1 | 0 | 1 | | |
| 1 | 1 | 0 | | |
| 1 | 1 | 1 | | |

(complete the last column by reference to the table for $x \Rightarrow y$ given above).

Draw eight diagrams to illustrate the eight rows of the table, and explain the difficulties which arise when you reach the sixth and seventh rows.

2. If $a$ is the proposition     $x = 1$
   and $b$ is the proposition   $x = 2$
   and $c$ is the proposition   $x^3 + 2x = 3x^2$

what is the meaning of the compound proposition

$$(a + b) \Rightarrow c?$$

Compile a truth table for this proposition, omitting the cases where $a = 1$ *and* $b = 1$ (why?) and giving values of $x$ which correspond to the cases where $a = 0$ *and* $b = 0$. (There is obviously some confusion here between the meaning of the symbols $a + b$ and the symbols $x^3 + 3x$, and also between the meaning of the symbols $a = 1$ and $x = 1$: for this reason other symbols are commonly used for conjunction and disjunction, rather than the symbols we use here, but nevertheless we retain our system for the remainder of this book.)

3. Construct a truth table for the proposition $a' + b$, and compare it with the table for $a \Rightarrow b$.

4. Write down in adjacent columns truth tables for the four propositions

$$a \Rightarrow b \qquad b \Rightarrow a \qquad a' \Rightarrow b' \qquad b' \Rightarrow a'$$

State which tables are identical.

If $a$ means "Jim has won a University place" and
  $b$ means "Jim has passed five GCE subjects",
translate the four propositions above into words. If the *first* proposition is *known* to be true, which of the others must also be true?

### Illogical reasoning

The implication sign is the mathematical expression of a common form of everyday remark. The analysis of such a remark carried out in Q.4 of the last exercise illustrates how it is possible to draw illogical conclusions even from a statement that we accept to be true. Unfortunately this sort of illogical reasoning is only too common. The confusion between $a \Rightarrow b$ and $b \Rightarrow a$ is the confusion between a statement and its *converse*.
The statement
  If he is in trouble with the law, then the police come for him
has as converse
  if the police come for him, then he is in trouble with the law.
Even if the first statement is accepted as true, it is quite illogical for inquisitive neighbours to assume the truth of the second statement.

The proposition $a' \Rightarrow b'$ is called the inverse of $a \Rightarrow b$. This again is not a logical consequence, but is frequently appealed to in everyday life. Too many people, starting from the (doubtful) statement

  If he is British, you can trust him

conclude that the inverse is also true:

  If he is not British, you can't trust him.

When we come to the last case, the comparison between $a \Rightarrow b$ and $b' \Rightarrow a'$, we are on firmer ground: these have the same truth table, and so are equivalent. The statement

  "if it is a square, it has four right angles"

is equivalent to the statement

  "if it has not four right angles, it is not a square".

On a more sophisticated plane, the statement

"if the velocity of light as observed by us depends on the velocity of the Earth through the ether, then light reflected from equal distances in different directions will return to us at different times"

led to an experiment at the end of the last century which surprisingly gave the negation of the second part of this proposition—in fact, the different rays of light returned at the same time. This in turn implied the negation of the first part—the velocity of light as observed by us does *not* depend on the velocity of the Earth through the ether: and this is one of the foundations of the theory of relativity.

### EXERCISE 4

1. $p =$ (tomorrow will be a fine day)
   $q =$ (we shall take a trip to the coast).

Write down the meaning of the following propositions in reasonable English:

   (a) $p \Rightarrow q$    (b) $q \Rightarrow p$    (c) $p' \Rightarrow q'$    (d) $q' \Rightarrow p'$

Assuming the truth of (a), which of the others are true?

2. $p =$ (this quadrilateral is a rhombus)
   $q =$ (this quadrilateral has perpendicular diagonals)

Repeat Q.1 for these new definitions of $p$ and $q$.

3. There is a theorem in the calculus which states that for numbers $a$ such that $f'(a) = 0$,

   if $f''(a)$ is negative, then $f(a)$ is a maximum of $f(x)$.

You may well know nothing whatever of the calculus, but you should be able to answer the following question:

   Does it follow from the above statement that if $f(a)$ is a maximum of $f(x)$, then $f''(a)$ is negative?

4. Let $a$ be the proposition  $p \Rightarrow q$
   Let $b$ be the proposition  $q \Rightarrow r$
   Let $c$ be the proposition  $p \Rightarrow r$

Complete the following truth table for the proposition

$$ab \Rightarrow c$$

| $p$ | $q$ | $r$ | $a$ | $b$ | $ab$ | $c$ | $ab \Rightarrow c$ |
|---|---|---|---|---|---|---|---|
| 0 | 0 | 0 | 1 | 1 | 1 | 1 | 1 |

What do you notice about the last column?

Such a proposition is called a *tautology*. A tautology is always true regardless of the truth of its elements: the one shown is the basis of the "chain of reasoning". We start at $p$, which leads us to $q$, which in turn leads us to $r$, and so on if necessary. If our reasoning is sound, that is, if $a$ and $b$ are both true (which means that $ab = 1$: note the four rows where this occurs), then the truth of $p$ leads us to the truth of both $q$ and $r$, and the falsity of $q$ or $r$ leads us to the conclusion that earlier propositions in the chain are false.

5. The proof given in *Sets and Logic 1*, Chapter IV, that $\sqrt{2}$ is not a rational number, is composed thus:

$a = (p$ and $q$ are integers with no common factor)
$b = (p^2/q^2 = 2)$

and the reasoning leads us to the conclusion that $p$ and $q$ do have a common factor, 2, that is

$$ab \Rightarrow a'$$

Compose a four-row truth table for this proposition.

Since the reasoning is sound, we must reject the case where 0 occurs in the last column. You will see that this means that $a$ and $b$ cannot be simultaneously true: hence there is no *rational* number whose square is 2.

### Equivalence

In the last section we were at pains to point out that

the proposition $a = (p \Rightarrow q)$
and its converse $b = (q \Rightarrow p)$

are not logically equivalent. If we wish to assert both $a$ and $b$, we use the symbolism

$$p \Leftrightarrow q$$

meaning that $p$ and $q$ are either both true or both false. We say that $p$ and $q$ are equivalent. From the definition, the truth table for $p \Leftrightarrow q$ is

| $p$ | $q$ | $p \Leftrightarrow q$ |
|-----|-----|-----------------------|
| 0   | 0   | 1                     |
| 0   | 1   | 0                     |
| 1   | 0   | 0                     |
| 1   | 1   | 1                     |

A simple example from Euclidean geometry illustrates the meaning of this symbol: if

$$p = \text{(this triangle has two equal sides)}$$
$$q = \text{(this triangle has two equal angles)}$$
$$\text{then} \quad p \Leftrightarrow q.$$

If either proposition is true, then so is the other, and if either is false, then the other is also.

Suppose $p$ = (the triangles $ABC$ and $DEF$ are congruent)

$q$ = (the triangles $ABC$ and $DEF$ are equal in area).

Then in Euclidean geometry

$$p \Rightarrow q.$$

We may translate this remark as

*p is a sufficient condition for q.*

If we are trying to show that the triangles are equal in area, and we manage to show that they are congruent, then that is sufficient: there is no more to be done. This type of phrase is very common in mathematics, and is not to be confused with the similar phrase

*q is a necessary condition for p.*

This second phrase means exactly the same as the first. It is another translation of $p \Rightarrow q$. You will see that the triangles must be equal in area in order that they be congruent: however, equality of area is not in itself enough to ensure congruence. $q$ is *not* a sufficient condition for $p$. Nor do two triangles have to be congruent in order to be equal in area. $p$ is *not* a necessary condition for $q$. This distinction between necessary and sufficient conditions is an important one, and must always be borne in mind.

Now it may happen that a condition is *both* necessary *and* sufficient. For a triangle to be isosceles, it is necessary that two angles should be equal, and this condition is also sufficient. Once we have shown that two angles are equal, there is no more to be done. This situation is the one described by the symbol $\Leftrightarrow$, and is sometimes stated using the phrase

"if and only if"

Thus: a triangle is isosceles if and only if two angles are equal.

1. $a = (x \in R,\ x^2 = 4x)$
   $b = (x = 4)$

Is $b$ a necessary condition for $a$? Is it a sufficient condition? Write down the relation between $a$ and $b$ using the symbol $\Rightarrow$.

2. In order that a quadrilateral should be a parallelogram, is the condition that its pairs of opposite sides be equal necessary, sufficient, or both?

3. In order that $\theta = 30°$, is the condition that $\sin \theta = 0 \cdot 5$ necessary, sufficient, or both?

4. $a = (p \Rightarrow q)$
   $b = (q \Rightarrow p)$

Show that $p \Leftrightarrow q$ and $ab$ are equivalent by completing the following truth table:

| $p$ | $q$ | $a$ | $b$ | $ab$ |
|-----|-----|-----|-----|------|
| 0   | 0   | 1   | 1   | 1    |

# Miscellaneous Examples

1. Show the following sets in a Venn diagram, placing the various sets in their correct relationship:

> $T$   The set of triangles
> $R$   the set of right-angled triangles
> $O$   the set of obtuse-angled triangles
> $I$   the set of isosceles triangles
> $E$   the set of equilateral triangles.

Describe the following sets, using a sketch if it appears helpful:

  (a) $R \cap I$     (b) $O \cap E$     (c) $I \cap O$     (d) $E \cap I$

2. Draw three intersecting ovals to represent the sets $X$, $Y$ and $Z$. Shade the set $X' \cup Z$. Now outline in colour the set $Y \cap (X' \cup Z)$. Finally, outline in another colour the set $X$. From your diagram complete the formula

$$X \cup [Y \cap (X' \cup Z)] =$$

Rewrite this formula using addition and multiplication symbols for $\cup$ and $\cap$. Hence prove your result by Boolean algebra.

3. Three coins, $A$, $B$ and $C$, were simultaneously tossed ten times. $A$ appeared heads on 6 occasions, $B$ appeared heads on 7 occasions, and $C$ appeared heads on 4 occasions. $A$ and $B$ both appeared heads simultaneously on 4 occasions. There was exactly one toss which yielded 3 heads. What is the maximum possible number of occasions on which exactly 2 heads appeared?

4. Draw a graph of the relation $A \cap B$, where

$$A = \{(x, y): x, y \in R, xy \leq 12\}$$
$$B = \{(x, y): x, y \in R, x^2 + y^2 \leq 16\}$$

State carefully the domain and range of each of the relations $A$ and $B$.

5. Use the graph of the relation $A$ in Q.4 to help solve the inequality $\dfrac{12}{x} \leq 4$

6. Draw a graph of the function $\{(x, y): x, y \in R, y = \dfrac{1}{2 - x}\}$

Use your graph to help solve the inequality $-1 \leq \dfrac{1}{2 - x} \leq 1$

7. Consider the inequality $\dfrac{2}{(x - 1)(x - 4)} \geq -1$

For what values of $x$ is the denominator of the left-hand side negative? Confining your attention for a moment to this set of values of $x$, multiply both sides of the inequality by the (negative) number $(x - 1)(x - 4)$ and hence find a set of numbers $x$ which satisfy the given inequality.

For what set of numbers $x$ is the denominator of the original inequality positive? For this set of numbers $x$, is the inequality satisfied or not? Give reasons for your answer. Write down the complete set of numbers $x$ which satisfy the given inequality.

8. Draw a graph of the relation $y = \cos x°$ $(0 \leq x \leq 180)$. Is this relation a function? What is the range? On a separate diagram draw a graph of the *inverse* relation, which is written $y° = \cos^{-1}x$. Is this relation a function? What is its domain? If you do not already know the definition of $\cos x°$ for $x > 180$, find out, and indicate how your graphs would continue if $x$ were allowed to take all values $\in R$ in the original relation. Would any of your answers to the questions now be different?

9. *Composition of functions.* The relation

$$\{(x, y): x, y \in R, y = x^2\}$$

is a function. An alternative way of writing this is

$$f \equiv x^2$$

where the reader is often left to interpret the domain from the context. Here, of course, $x \in R$. If we select a first element $x$, say 3, then the second element, $y$, is 9. We can say that 9 is the *image* of 3 *under f*, and we write

$$f(3) = 9$$

Write down the numbers $f(2), f(0), f(-1/2), f(y)$.

Consider now the function

$$g \equiv x + 1$$

Write down the numbers $g(5), g(-4)$

We have already seen that $f(3) = 9$. Now $g(9) = 9 + 1 = 10$.

Here we have first found the image of 3 under $f$, and then found the image of this number, 9, under $g$. This may be written

$$g.f(3) = 10$$

Write down the numbers $g.f(2)$, $g.f(4)$, and write down a formula for $g.f(x)$.

Since $f$ and $g$ are functions, $x$ will have a unique image $y$ under $f$, and this $y$ will have a unique image $z$ under $g$, so that $x$ has a unique image $z$ under the relation $g.f$. Thus $g.f$ is a function, called the *composite* of the functions $g$ and $f$. Show that the . symbol here is non-commutative by finding $f.g(2)$, $f.g(4)$, and writing down a formula for $f.g(x)$, then comparing with the answers to the similar questions above.

10. If $\quad f \equiv 1 - x$

$\qquad$ and $g \equiv 1/x$

find the numbers $f.g(3)$, $g.f(3)$, and investigate $g.f(1)$. Write down formulae for $f.g(x)$ and $g.f(x)$.

11. If $\quad f \equiv$ is the father of

use a similar phrase to describe the function $f.f$ (which may be written $f^2$).

12. If $\quad f \equiv x^2$

$\qquad g \equiv 2x$

$\qquad h \equiv \sin x°$

write down a formula for $f.g(x)$ and another for $g.h(x)$. What is the number $f.(g.h)(30)$? What is the number $(f.g).h(30)$? Do you think this operation of composition of functions is associative?

Find the numbers $f.g.h(5)$, $g.h.f(5)$, $h.g.f(5)$.

13. *Logarithms*. We start with some definitions:

(a) If $x \in Z^+$, $y = 10^x$ is defined by the rule

$\qquad y = 10 \times 10 \times \ldots 10$ ($x$ factors)

If $x = 0$, $y = 10^x$ is defined to be 1.

If $x \in Z^+$ $y = 10^{-x}$ is defined to be $1/10^x$ e.g. $10^{-2} = \frac{1}{10^2} = \frac{1}{100}$

If $x \in Q$, so that $x = a/b$, $a \in Z$, $b \in Z^+$

$\qquad y$ is defined to be the positive real value of $\sqrt[b]{10^a}$

$\qquad$ e.g. $10^{-\frac{2}{3}} = \sqrt[3]{10^{-2}} = \sqrt[3]{\frac{1}{100}}$

Note that for $x \in Q$, $10^x$ may be irrational.

If $y = 10^x$, then $x$ is called the logarithm of $y$ to the base 10

$\qquad$ (written $x = \log_{10} y$).

More generally, for any $a \in R$,
$$y = a^x \Leftrightarrow x = \log_a y.$$

Draw a graph of $y = 2^x$, taking as domain the set

$$\{-2, -1\tfrac{1}{2}, -1, \ldots 1\tfrac{1}{2}, 2\}$$

Does your graph indicate that there is a one-to-one correspondence between the domain and range of the relation

$$x = \log_2 y?$$

Does your graph prove it?

What difficulties of definition arise for the relation

$$y = 2^x$$

if $x$ is irrational? (This difficulty is a very real one.) *Assuming* that this difficulty has been surmounted, and that it is permissible to join up the isolated points of your graph with a smooth curve, indicating that the relation $y = 2^x$ is a one-to-one correspondence between two sets of real numbers, state carefully the domain and range of this relation.

|   | 1 | 2 | 3 | 4 | 5 |
|---|---|---|---|---|---|
| 1 |   |   |   |   |   |
| 2 | 2 | 4 | 0 | 2 | 4 |
| 3 | 3 | 0 | 3 | 0 | 3 |
| 4 |   |   |   |   |   |
| 5 |   |   |   |   |   |

14. Complete the adjoining multiplication table "modulo 6": that is, each product of two numbers is replaced by its remainder on division by 6. Does this table satisfy all the conditions for a group?

15. Complete a table for the products of the numbers 1, 2, 3, 4, 5, 6 modulo 7. Does this table satisfy all the conditions for a group?

16. Define functions as follows:

$$f \equiv 1 - x$$
$$g \equiv \frac{1}{x}$$

and $p \equiv f.g = 1 - \dfrac{1}{x} = \dfrac{x-1}{x}$

$q \equiv g.f = \dfrac{1}{1-x}$

$r \equiv g.p = \dfrac{x}{x-1}$

Add to this list the *identity* function

$$i \equiv x$$

and we may compose a "multiplication table" for the six functions $i, f, g, p, q, r$. For example,

$$p.g = \dfrac{\dfrac{1}{x} - 1}{\dfrac{1}{x}} = 1 - x = f$$

Part of the table is given below: complete it.

|   | i | f | g | p | q | r |
|---|---|---|---|---|---|---|
| i | i | f | g | p | q | r |
| f | f |   | p |   |   |   |
| g | g | q |   | r |   |   |
| p | p |   | f |   |   |   |
| q | q |   |   |   |   |   |
| r | r |   |   |   |   |   |

Does the table satisfy all the conditions necessary to form a group?

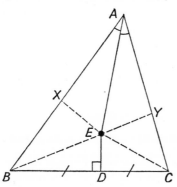

17. In the given diagram, $ABC$ is a triangle in which $AB \neq AC$ (assumption $p$), $DE$ is the perpendicular bisector of the line-segment $BC$, $AE$ is the bisector of the angle $A$, and these two lines meet at a point $E$

inside the triangle (assumption $q$). $EX \perp AB$, $EY \perp AC$. Explain why the following pairs of triangles are congruent:

$$BED \text{ and } CED \qquad \text{(a)}$$
$$AEX \text{ and } AEY \qquad \text{(b)}$$
$$BEX \text{ and } CEY \qquad \text{(c)}$$

$$\text{Now (b)} \Rightarrow AX = AY \text{ (h)}$$
$$\text{and } \text{ (c)} \Rightarrow BX = CY \text{ (k)}$$

Further, (h) *and* (k) $\Rightarrow AB = AC$, which contradicts assumption $(p)$, and so we have the chain of reasoning

$$pq \Rightarrow p'$$

Complete the following truth table for this function:

| $p$ | $q$ | $pq$ | $p'$ | $pq \Rightarrow p'$ |
|-----|-----|------|------|---------------------|
| 0 | 0 | 0 | 1 | 1 |
| 0 | 1 |   |   |   |
| 1 | 0 |   |   |   |
| 1 | 1 |   |   |   |

If we accept that it is possible to find a triangle with two unequal sides, we must take $p = 1$. If also we accept that our reasoning is sound, we must take $(pq \Rightarrow p') = 1$. What is the value of $q$ in the row corresponding to these values? Wherein lies the fallacy?

18. A committee of four members, $A$, $B$, $C$ and $D$, passes resolutions by a simple majority vote, except that in the event of a tie the chairman $A$ has the casting vote. Voting is to be carried out by a system such that each member presses the switch in front of him if he is supporting the motion, and a light is to appear on an indicator if the resolution is passed, but will not appear if a resolution is defeated. Design a circuit which will do this.

19. On p. 34 we met the formula

$$P(A \cup B) = P(A) + P(B) - P(A \cap B)$$

which was deduced from a similar formula for the number of elements in the set $A \cup B$, written $n(A \cup B)$. By drawing a Venn diagram for three intersecting sets $A$, $B$ and $C$, and writing arbitrary positive integers in the spaces to indicate the numbers of elements in the various subsets, verify the formula

$$n(A \cup B \cup C) = n(A) + n(B) + n(C)$$
$$- [n(B \cap C) + n(C \cap A) + n(A \cap B)]$$
$$+ n(A \cap B \cap C)$$

Write down the corresponding probability formula.

The problem that follows is a simplified version of a famous one which has appeared in many forms:

A man has just written three letters and is in a hurry to catch the post. He pushes the letters into their envelopes without even bothering to check that the letters and envelopes are correctly paired. What is the probability that at least one letter is in the correct envelope?

We may denote the envelopes by the letters $A$, $B$ and $C$, and we may also without confusion denote by the letter $A$ the event that envelope $A$ contains its correct letter. Using this notation, what is $P(A)$? What is $P(A) + P(B) + P(C)$? We now move on to the last term: how many possible arrangements are there of the letters in the envelopes? How many of these place every letter in its correct envelope? What is $P(A \cap B \cap C)$?

Now consider $P(B \cap C)$. This is the probability that $B$ and $C$ both contain the correct letter: but in this case, $A$ must also contain the correct letter, and so all three are correct, and this probability we have already calculated. Finally, by substituting all these various values in your formula, calculate the probability required in the original question.

20. See if you can solve the previous question for the case when the man has written *four* letters.

# Hints and Answers

## Chapter I

Exercise 1: (2) The last three symbols in the column are 1s. (3), (7) Find the formula in the Appendix.

Exercise 2: If the standard pattern for the tables as used in the text, the final columns should read: (1) 1, 1, 1, 0   (4) 0, 1, 1, 0.

Exercise 3: (1) (a) $x + xy \; (= x)$   (d) $xy'$   (f) $xy + x'y'$   (2) (b) $x'$   (e) $y$
(3) (b) $(x + z)(y + z)$   (f) $(x + y')(x' + y)$   (4) (b) $x' + y$   (e) $x'y' + x'z$
(5) $x + y(x' + z)(= x + y)$   (6) $xy + x'(y + z')(y' + z)$   (7), (8) The final column reads 1, 0, 0, 1, 0 ,0, 1, 1   (10) $xyz$.

## Chapter II

Exercise 1. (1) $x'y + xy' + xy$. Factorise the last two terms, then factorise again.
(2)

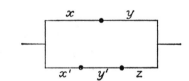

(3) One possibility is $x(yz + y'z') + x'(yz' + y'z)$.

Exercise 3: (1)

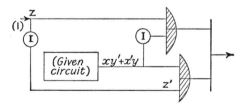

(2) See the circuit on p. 29.

Exercise 5: (2) $p = x'y'z + x'yz' + xy'z' + xyz$. This is the same as one of the digits in a full adder: which? $q$ resembles very closely the other digit of a full adder.

77

## Chapter III

Exercise 2: (1) (b) $\frac{1}{2}$ (e) $\frac{5}{6}$ (f) $\frac{1}{6}$ (2) $\frac{1}{12}$, $\frac{1}{6}$, $\frac{1}{4}$ (b) $\frac{7}{12}$.

Exercise 3: (1) (c) $\frac{1}{9}$ (d) 0 (f) $\frac{1}{4}$ (2) The pairs $(x, y)$: $x = y$ are no longer sample points (b) $\frac{2}{15}$ (f) $\frac{1}{5}$ (4) $n(P \times P \times P) = 8$ (b) $\frac{3}{8}$ (5) $\frac{3}{8}$ (6) The probability that the hidden side has the same colour as the exposed side is $\frac{2}{3}$.

Exercise 4: (1) and (2) both describe pairs of dependent events (3) $\frac{1}{6} \times \frac{1}{2} = \frac{1}{12}$ (4) $\frac{1}{8} \times \frac{2}{13} = \frac{1}{52}$.

Exercise 5: (2) $\frac{3}{8}$.

## Chapter IV

Exercise 1: (1) The images are $(1, -1)$, $(2, -1)$, $(3, -1)$, $(2, -2)$, $(2, 0)$, $(2, 1)$ (4) All points map onto the line $\{(p, q) : q = 2p\}$

Exercise 2: All but (b), (h), (i) are equivalence relations (if by convention, in (e), a line is considered to be parallel to itself).

Exercise 3: (1) Interchange the rows and columns 3 and 4 (2) lacks closure (3) is a group.

Exercise 4: (2) Apply the definitions strictly (remember not to assume familiar properties of "fractions" not yet proved) and then appeal to the axioms for integers (3) Consider $a + 0 = a$ and multiply both sides by $a$. Then use the cancellation axiom for addition (4) $ab = 0 \iff ab = a.0 \iff b = 0$ (if $a \neq 0$). Similarly show that $a = 0$ (if $b \neq 0$). This proves that for $ab = 0$, at least one of $a$, $b$ is zero.

Exercise 5: (2) (a) is the only total ordering (c) is the only equivalence relation. There is no partial ordering.

Exercise 6: (2) $\frac{3}{3}$; 6. An objection may be made that some rational numbers are counted more than once: if we wish to use assumptions such as $\frac{1}{2} = \frac{2}{4}$, it is a simple enough matter to strike out $\frac{2}{4}$ and all subsequent equivalent rationals in the array.

## Chapter V

Exercise 1: Only (6) and (7) are definitely not propositions. There is room for argument about (1).

Exercise 2: (4) I should not like both to swim and to play tennis today (6) I should like either to go swimming or to play tennis, but not both.

Exercise 3: (1) Trouble arises in the sixth and seventh rows because, given $p$, $q$ and $r$ each imply the other (4) $b' \Rightarrow a'$.

Exercise 5: (1) Consider $x = 0$ (2) Both (3) Consider sin 150°.

# Appendix

## THE LAWS OF BOOLEAN ALGEBRA

1. $A + B = B + A$      $AB = BA$      (Commutative)
2. $A + (B + C) = (A + B) + C$    $A(BC) = (AB)C$    (Associative)
3. $A(B + C) = AB + AC$    $A + BC = (A + B)(A + C)$
                                                        (Distributive)

4. $A + A = A$      $AA = A$
5. $A + A' = 1$      $AA' = 0$
6. $1' = 0$      $0' = 1$
7. $1 + A = 1$      $0A = 0$
8. $0 + A = A$      $1A = A$
9. $(A + B)' = A'B'$      $(AB)' = A' + B'$      (De Morgan's
10. $(A')' = A$                                                 Laws)

Note that of the twelve laws not involving complements, only four are not true in ordinary algebra. These are (4), the second part of (3) and the first part of (7).